MADE IN
HUNGARY

A Life Forged by History

Maria Krenz

DONNER PUBLISHING

Donner Publishing
1919 Grove St.
Boulder, CO 80302

LCCN 2009937416
ISBN-10 0-9825393-0-4
ISBN-13 978-0-9825393-0-9
Copyright information available upon request.

Cover Design: Graphics by Manjari
Photo of Chain Bridge by Péter Róoz, Budapest
Interior Design: J. L. Saloff
Typography: Adobe Jenson Pro, Aquiline

v. 1.0
First Edition, 2009
Printed on acid free paper.

*To my parents and sisters, and to all
who wander the world in search of belonging.*

Contents

Acknowledgments

This book was written on my heart a long time ago, unbeknownst to me. Unable to make peace with my past and my homeland, I took what I thought was my last trip to Hungary in 1989. It was a return to Hungary in 2002 with my friend and partner, Mary Hey, that gave me the courage to unearth my past and to revisit places and feelings I couldn't have faced alone. Her steadfast support and sympathy gave me the courage finally to put my story into words, and with that find understanding and healing. My deepest gratitude goes to her for that and for her careful reading and helpful comments, and for never failing to urge me on.

I am also indebted to many friends who encouraged me along the way and read the work in progress—Dagny Scott, Christopher Braider, Ellen Gault, Kirbie Knutson, Sarah Krakoff, Roberta Krakoff, Ellen Orleans, and Mimi Wesson. My deepest thanks to all of you for your valuable help.

Preface

I am a sixty-five year old Quaker American, who was born a Hungarian Jew. One day as my sixtieth birthday approached, I looked in the mirror, trying once again to figure out who that person looking back at me was. For an instant—revelation or hallucination—I saw clearly stamped on the forehead in the mirror "made in Hungary." Forty-five of my years have been spent in the United States. Only the first thirteen were spent in Hungary. So why the stamp?

This book was born from two impulses. Without the first it couldn't have been written. Without the second, I had no reason to write it. My first impulse was to find out what is it in my childhood, what is it about Hungary that so completely formed me, to understand my unrequited love affair with my country of birth, a country that had never wanted me and never considered me or my people real Hungarians. I love the United States, the ideals it stands for, its unequivocal welcome to me. I feel profoundly grateful and loyal to it. But it is Hungary's landscape, Hungary's music, Hungary's foods, and the beauty of Budapest that evoke the deepest quivering in my soul. It is a resonance that is love but also hate, both longing and bitterness. I decided to delve into this schizophrenic relationship. Why does my heart delight when I see a Hungarian name, yet I am filled with fear when I see the Hungarian national coat-of-arms tattooed on a young man's arm? The idea that I could find answers to all my questions was naïve. As memories came to me first slowly and then sometimes like a rushing torrent—never chronologically—I puzzled together the pieces of the jigsaw of my family's and my life, through the Holocaust and the years under communism. Along the way I edged closer to making my peace with the past.

The second impulse, just as compelling, was to share with my friends and my American compatriots something about the story of twentieth century Hungary, that basin of land in the middle of Europe—to some Central Europe, to others Eastern Europe—about which so little has registered in this country. And why would Americans know more about it? Hungary is one of more than a hundred countries and not very significant in the world arena. Yet widening our understanding of those dozens of countries that make up our twenty-first century world has to be worthwhile. This was something I could contribute to my adopted country.

The recitation of historical facts is not very illuminating, often boring, and easily forgettable. Here, instead, I have chosen to tell a personal story steeped in history. Some chapters are more personal than others. Others include more history, delving into the context more deeply. My hope is that together, this braid of two strands presents a lively portrait of a people, a country, and a time—the

Holocaust and communism—that still raises many questions in most of our minds.

I offer this book with gratitude to the country that took me in with open arms and heart.

My Holocaust

I was born during a bombing raid on Budapest on April 24, 1944. My mother went into sudden hard labor six weeks early. My father begged and begged and finally the ambulance came despite the wail of the sirens warning everyone to take shelter. I took my first breath in the hospital's air raid shelter with the help of my father's cousin Andrew Zágon, who was a doctor. My timing was providential, for a few weeks later Jews would no longer be allowed at any hospital.

How can anyone write about that first year of life? I know the details of mine because my mother wrote her recollections when we were able to return home. But the true memories are embedded in my cells and inscribed in my soul by her reliving that year over and over again. Trembling, near hysterical, withdrawn into her inner vision of the horrors that touched her, my mother would go over them again and again during the years of my childhood.

Just a few weeks before my birth, on March 19, 1944, Germany invaded its reluctant ally, Hungary. There had been no armed resistance to the invasion, for the country after all had officially joined Hitler's war in June 1941. It was clear that the war was going badly for the Axis. Hitler's spy network knew that Hungary's head of state, Regent Horthy, was attempting to make a separate peace with the Allies. Also, the German Nazi machine grew more and more frustrated with Hungary's insistence that it would deal with the "Jewish Question" on its own terms and with its failure to deliver the Jews to the camps. Hence the invasion.

But at least the Holocaust came rather late to Hungary. Despite being branded and discriminated against, taken to forced labor camps, and reviled in the press, the bulk of Hungarian Jewry survived the first three and a half years of the war while the "Final Solution" was carried out all around them. Most of the Jews, still patriotic and insistently Magyar (Hungarian), were convinced that what was happening to the Jews wherever the Germans had reached would not, could not, happen to them in civilized Hungary. As Elie Wiesel put it, "Budapest was still a very quiet, peaceful city until 1944.... The Jews of Budapest lived in a strange hallucination."

The invasion put an end to that. The killing of Hungarian Jews started in earnest, with the willing cooperation of the new Hungarian government and the people. Maybe because there was still resistance to it by some of the non-Jewish population of Budapest, the roundup started in the countryside. Only much later did we find out that over a six-week period about 440,000 souls, virtually the entire Jewish population outside of Budapest, were deported to the camps. From late March to mid-May the deportation was so efficient that the crematoria in Auschwitz-Birkenau couldn't cope. Special ditches were dug to burn the thousands of Hungarian Jews the ovens couldn't handle. Yet Budapest was still more or less intact.

In Budapest an order was promulgated on March 31st, 1944, three weeks before I was born, compelling Jews to wear a six-pointed, canary-yellow 4x4 inch star on the top left side of their clothing. Catholic authorities worked to exempt Jews who had converted to Christianity on the grounds that it would be heresy for them to wear the symbol of Judaism. Yielding to Catholic pressure, converted Jews who were married to "pure" Christians—that is, Aryans—were exempt.

Those wearing the yellow star were fair game, unprotected by the law. My mother, almost seven months pregnant, was scared to go far into the city and stayed as much as possible in our little neighborhood on the outskirts of Buda. Although our neighborhood seemed far away and quiet, from further in the city came stories of young thugs jeering and spitting at old women wearing yellow stars, of shoving, pushing, and kicking old men, of shooting younger ones, of gang rapes.

There were days when my parents had no choice but to venture deeper into the city. Even though they experienced no physical harm, they were forced to pass the omnipresent hate-filled posters inviting, inciting the population to violence and revenge. The posters, all grotesque caricatures, varied. Some depicted Jews as deformed and evil sub-humans who stole the wealth of the nation and left the real Hungarians unemployed and poor, others as Bolsheviks, yet others as monsters who defiled the purity of

the Hungarian race. My father, always a Hungarian patriot, was heartbroken. Mother was petrified. Until then, being Jewish had been an abstraction to her. It was her ancestry but not her religion. Her family converted when she was fourteen and she had become a devout Catholic. She had married another converted Jew. Her family and her friends were cultured, idealistic people who shared that ancestry but also were not particularly religious. She had never lived in a Jewish neighborhood. Pogroms were something terrible but remote, something that those poor uneducated and unfortunate Jews of far-away Galicia experienced, not the assimilated Catholics of Jewish roots living in cosmopolitan Budapest. But by this time being Jewish was declared to be a matter of race, not of religion. Always excitable and sensitive, and now fearing for her and her baby's life, seeing the posters, and feeling surrounded by hate, my mother didn't really know anymore who she was. She was left without identity and without the support of the Jewish community, who tried to look after their own as much as possible. There was nothing left but the family.

I was a ten-day old, barely four-pound preemie, when the Nazis came to our apartment to announce "the Jews have to get out." They gave us a week. When Father implored them, "What about my newborn daughter?" one replied, "The world doesn't need any more Jews. If you make a

---

Opposite: *Two anti-Jewish posters. The top one reads: "Shame on you! You bought from a Jew again!" It gives the address of the Arrow Cross party. The bottom one refers to the Allied bombing of Budapest and is signed by the True Hungary movement: "An eye for an eye! For every Hungarian life a hundred Jews!"*

fuss, we'll throw you out now and you'll take nothing with you."

Where to go? Grandmami, my mother's mother, lived on the busy Margit Boulevard leading to the Margit Bridge over the Danube, and was too frightened to leave her apartment, but had not been evicted yet. We left all of our possessions with a friendly older Aryan lady and her daughter who lived in our building, and gathering some clothes and a few things, made our way to Grandmami's apartment. It felt more dangerous there because it was closer to the city center where there was more activity, but it had the advantage that my mother's older sister Trudi had an apartment on the top floor of the same large apartment house. Being the converted widow of an Aryan, she was exempt from wearing a yellow star and able to go shopping without fear and without being restricted by the ever-stricter curfews limiting when Jews were allowed on the streets. She became our lifeline.

At Grandmami's apartment the challenges of daily life left little time and energy to think. Mother nursed me, hauled large buckets of water from the bathroom tub to the stove to heat up to wash clothes and diapers, and tried to feed us with what Trudi or my father managed to scrounge up. With the German occupation of Hungary, Allied forces had begun bombing the city on April 2nd, three weeks before my birth. Several times, day and night, everybody in the six-story building had to run to the air raid shelter. In between, despite the danger, Father went out to try to find food and coal. Perhaps he also wanted to get out of the house, to stop feeling impotent. Fifty-six years old to

Mother's thirty-seven, he had never felt out of control before, except perhaps at the death of his first wife. One day he came back carrying a leaflet picked up on the street, the leaflet demanding the life of one hundred Jews for every Christian killed in the Allied bombing. Those posters. That leaflet. The country he so loved and fought for. The people he so trusted. How could he have been so wrong? How could everything he believed in become a lie? What was there to hold on to?

Our stay at Grandmami's lasted only five weeks. Mid-June a new decree came: all Jews had to move into buildings that the government designated with yellow stars. Which buildings? Nobody knew. There were no empty buildings. Houses were designated and then undesignated. Confusion reigned. Ironically, Christians ordered to move out of the designated buildings had yet one more thing to blame the Jews for. Rather than designate a group of houses together, the occupation's puppet government decided to scatter yellow-star buildings next to important government and military buildings, with the idea that this would deter the Allies from bombing those buildings. It didn't.

My father finally found a room in a large yellow-star house on Nádor Street in Pest. The three of us, plus Grandmami and Trudi's partner, Miklós, who was also Jewish, moved in. It was the old windowless dining room of an ancient apartment, utterly filthy. Eighteen people, including several young children, crowded into the two bedroom apartment. Mostly strangers to each other, some people were helpful, but there was much squabbling, as they were all vying for space. My mother, a fanatic of cleanliness, was convinced that I would die of some disease picked up from the dirt and people surrounding us. She directed her energies to keeping a square meter around me clean.

At least this impossible task allowed her to focus her mind on something other than the rumors swirling around us, rumors that turned out to be surprisingly accurate. Most, if not all the Jews from the countryside had been rounded up and deported from the provinces in sealed cattle cars. Children were murdered wholesale, crying babies smashed against the pavement. Then the roundups came closer, to the outskirts of Budapest. The Jews were taken

My mother in the shared kitchen of
the yellow star house on Nádor Street.

from Pesterzsébet, Csepel, Ujpest. The noose was tightening. Mother was beside herself, pacing around, bursting out with what must have been on many minds in that crowded place: How long before it is our turn? When will they take us away in a sealed wagon? What will happen to my baby? The bombing continued and we spent more and more time in the air raid shelter, even more crowded than upstairs. But as frightening as the air raids were, they were our promise too. Maybe the Allies would win in time to save us.

In July other rumors reached us. The deportations had been halted in response to protest from the King of Sweden and the Pope! We might live if we survived. The Allied bombings grew more intense and frequent. One evening, while everybody was crowded in the cellar, the apartment house received several direct hits. Plaster rained on people's heads. The explosions continued. Father and Mother, sure the next hit would cause a cave in, embraced each other over my basket. But silence followed, the sortie was over. People from the cellar of the adjacent house pulled everyone out and over to their cellar for the night. As light dawned and people ventured out they found just parts of the house remaining, gaping holes, rooms half-exposed, their other half blown away. Where to next? We needed a place right then and finding another yellow-star place with space, or with people willing to crowd themselves further to take in others, was very difficult.

Father's cousin Andrew lived not too far away. With a shortage of "pure" physicians, the Aryan population needed some of the Jewish doctors to continue practicing and so they were exempted from many of the restrictions. To be found harboring Jews, however, would be the end of him. After frantic searching, he found a patient of his who was willing to keep us for a couple of nights, during which my father found us another place. They found Grandmami, who had pneumonia and was quite ill, a place with her sister-in-law in another yellow-star house. Miklós went with Trudi back to their apartment, at her insistence, despite the danger to her if he were to be found.

We went to Pozsonyi Street, to another crowded and dark room. Another jammed cellar during air raids. But there was a walkway ringing each floor around the inner courtyard from which you entered the apartment and Mother was happy to take me out to it when there was a quiet moment to absorb some sunshine. The deportations seemed indeed to have been halted, and everybody breathed a little easier. Some dared to be hopeful. My mother even found the courage to take me out to the nearby banks of the Danube. Despite being a small preemie and all that was happening, I was healthy and growing. But probably from all the anxiety, Mother's milk dried up, so now they had the added challenge of finding milk or other food for me.

People's hopes that the worst was over and we might have survived peaked for a brief moment in the morning of October 15th, when Regent Horthy, whom for some reason the Germans had not yet deposed, proclaimed an armistice. Everyone was jubilant. Jews removed their yellow stars and went outside. But the jubilation was premature. Hitler's annoyance and frustration over the failure to complete the "final solution" program was matched by his anger at the Hungarians' attempts to extricate themselves from the war. The Germans kidnapped Horthy's son and to save his son's life, Horthy accepted the appointment of Szálasy, the leader of the Arrow-Cross party (the Hungarian Nazi party) as the head of the government. The reprieve for Budapest's Jews was over.

Right away, on the morning of the fifteenth, Trudi came to where we were staying, proposing that we come back to the apartment house on Margit Boulevard, not to Grandmami's old apartment, since no Jews were allowed, but to hide in her sixth-floor apartment. The atelier where Miklós, a well-known European artist, had painted and she had sculpted had received a full hit a couple of days before, and most of their art had been destroyed, but the apartment house was intact. Always decisive, she had already collected Grandmami. Father agreed that it might be a good time to get out of the yellow-star house. Now our only hope was that the Russians were very near, that Budapest was nearly surrounded. It must be just a matter of days, and maybe there wouldn't be time for us to be discovered at Trudi's.

Her apartment, long and narrow like a train car, contained a last room, which could be somewhat concealed by an armoire. There we stayed, not for days but for six harrowing weeks in terror of being discovered, in terror of being hit by a bomb, and starved not just for food but for information of the outside world. Every ring of the doorbell brought panic. If it turned out to be just the mailman or a friend, Trudi would casually whistle a tune to let us know as soon as possible to stay hidden but that it was OK. I was the biggest danger to us all. Keeping me quiet, repressing a six-month-old baby's natural desire to explore and express herself, was Mother's main task. She would walk up and down during endless hours, humming very low to entertain me or get me to sleep. When Trudi had to leave the apartment we could not make a sound so that those living below wouldn't hear someone moving around. Once Mother just had tiptoed to the kitchen to warm up some food for me when the doorbell rang and kept ringing until finally someone on the other side gave up. The long minutes pressed against the wall, hardly daring to breathe and praying that I wouldn't make a sound in my basket in the end room were etched in her memory of horrors. She dredged this up time and again, together with so many of the more awful moments of those six weeks.

Even in the chaos of moving from place to place without any notice, in some mysterious way family and friends kept an eye on each other. As if an invisible Ariadne's thread lay over the community, if you were looking for someone near and dear, you could find them. Father always kept track of his two adult daughters, Eva and Márta, whose mother had died several years before my parents met. He knew that Márta somehow managed to secure a place in one of the Swiss safe houses. Eva's husband, Willie, was taken away. The family prayed that since he was young and strong, he would not be killed but only forced to work in one of the labor camps. Eva and little Gábor shared a room in another yellow-star house with some of our Fleischl cousins. But after October 15th it became clear that the yellow star houses were all targets for collecting Jews toward the concentration camps and Eva, too, left. She found us at Trudi's apartment and asked to hide with us. That would mean not only another adult but a sixteen-month-old active boy. Father's most terrible moment came. He had to decide. Could he afford to increase the risk of discovery of his wife and baby? Could he stand to send away his daughter and grandson to let them fend for themselves? The man who had up to then always felt that he knew what was right had to face that there was no right choice. God only knows how he felt and reasoned, but he sent them away, giving Eva some papers that he thought might help get her into one of the safe houses established by the Swiss and the Swedes. His decision may have saved all of our lives, but it broke something in the soul of both of them that would never heal.

One evening during the second week of our stay, three Arrow Cross thugs, one of them with blood on his overcoat, came to Trudi's apartment. Gesticulating with their revolvers, they told Trudi that someone had informed them that there were Jews in the apartment. They pushed their way in and ransacked the place. They found the five of us. Triumphantly they demanded certificates of baptism. Grandmami, trembling, showed them hers. Then a miracle happened. They could hardly read, so they saw it was a certificate of baptism but could not see that the date was decades later than the birth date. Then they demanded Father's. Father had given his certificate to Eva, so he tried the ruse of giving them mine. One of them caught on. "But this is a child's certificate." Summoning a presence of mind from his years of iron discipline, my father replied, "I have already shown you mine." The miracle held. They didn't pursue it further. Trudi's partner, Miklós, however, was an active Jew and had no baptismal certificate. The three were triumphant. "So you did have a Jew!" One of them wanted to take also Trudi away for harboring a Jew. Mercifully, Grandmami's crying and pleading moved another one to relent and convince the others to leave with just poor Miklós. The possibility of another raid, next time with less luck, hung over our heads every minute of the weeks following.

The Allied bombings increased daily. We were on the sixth floor, the top floor of the building. While everyone else could go to the cellar for shelter, we couldn't because we weren't supposed to be there. So we had to stay on the top floor, where we surely would be killed if a bomb hit. During the attacks, the bombs whistled around us, followed by explosions that shook the apartment, followed by the sound of mortar and brick clattering close by. The anti-aircraft battery kept firing directly over the roof above us. Mother, Father, and Grandmami would kneel, holding hands so they could die together, and with their bodies they sheltered the laundry basket that was my bed, so if the ceiling came crashing in it wouldn't crush me first or separately from them. Mother, hysterical and at the end of her endurance, tried several times just opening the gas stove and ending it all, as her aunt and uncle had done in Vienna when the Germans took over Austria in 1938. Father kept restraining her, telling her she had no right to dispose of my life as well.

So the days passed, sometimes with sprinklings of hope but mostly of despair. Trudi gathered rumors and information in her forays. She found out about friends and acquaintances who had been herded off to no one knew where and about Uncle Rezsö shot into the Danube. Yes, the Russians were really, really close, but the thugs of the Arrow Cross were on a rampage. They were determined not to leave any Jews alive for the Russians to save. They lined up hundreds and hundreds and shot them into the Danube, sometimes first stripping them naked. Other times they chained them together, shot one, forcing him to drag the others live into the rushing icy water.

The Arrow Cross entered the safe houses established by Sweden, Switzerland, and the Red Cross and took away people or tortured them to death. A large ghetto

The memorial erected where the Jews were shot into the Danube in the last weeks of the Holocaust. (Photo by Péter Roóz, Budapest)

was built—with Jewish labor—by walling in the mostly Jewish neighborhood that surrounded the Dohány Street Synagogue. Everyone caught and not executed or still living in yellow-star houses outside the perimeter was herded to the newly created ghetto. The prevailing opinion was that the ghetto would be blown up before the Nazis were forced out of Budapest.

Rumors and facts blended into a giant morass of fear. We were paralyzed, just waiting to be found and taken away. Aryan refugees from the provinces taken over by the Russians streamed into Budapest and the government requisitioned apartments to house them. How long before they come to Trudi's to take over her apartment and find us there?

Help came unexpectedly. Providence wore two faces: that of Trudi's friend Mary Kállay and our old housekeeper, Juszti, who kept in touch with Trudi. Mary came and went about in the city with her false identity papers, defying bombs and Nazis, trying to help others. She convinced us to leave Trudi's apartment posing as Aryan refugees from the provinces. She helped us figure out how to do it. Trudi still had all the personal documents of her deceased Aryan husband, Gene. She gave Gene's identity paper to my father, and her own to my mother, keeping for herself the papers from Gene's deceased sister-in-law. Grandmami posed as Gene's mother. The only hitch was, who was I? Here Juszti came to the rescue, talking her brother into giving her the papers of his illegitimate baby a month older than I. I became Anna Fabo, the adopted child of my parents.

Mary found an attorney, a trusted friend, who found someone who wanted to rent an apartment to responsible refugees, and then he procured a stamped, blank identity card from Kassa, a city in what was northern Hungary (Slovakia after World War I). The city had a large Hungarian population, and as the Russians occupied it, thousands fled to Budapest. The next task was to leave Trudi's apartment undetected and get ourselves to the apartment in the big building on Közraktár Street on the Pest side (Budapest was divided by the Danube into Buda and Pest). Tiptoeing in the darkness the family left the apartment one by one, allowing some time between. Juszti was carrying me. We met up on the street in our new roles: Dr. Jenö (Gene) Kovács and family, refugees from Kassa, on their way to their new apartment. Juszti's brother met us with a cart carrying some bedding and food he found for us. There were many terrible people in Budapest in 1944, but there were many good ones too.

We spent the last four months before liberation in our new identities. Juszti stayed with us some of the time, helping out and bucking up my mother, who could barely keep a hold on herself. As things improved, the terrible experiences of the prior eight months caught up with her. And of course, the fear of discovery was always present. She had never been to Kassa. How to dissemble if someone asked her something? Adding to her fear was that my father might be conscripted. Hitler commanded that the German—and Hungarian—army fight to the last man. In a desperate last ditch they were conscripting even people in their fifties. As Gene Kovács, Father was two years younger than his real age. As a 54-year-old Aryan refugee from Kassa, he was subject to military service.

Other than the fear of discovery, we experienced the last few months of the war as did the rest of the besieged population of Budapest; hungry, cold, and afraid. But not quite. To my parents' ears the ever closer sounding rumble of Russian cannon fire was a promise of survival. To others around them it signified the defeat of not just Germany but of Hungary, inexorably tied as they were. When Christmas came, my first, in the bomb shelter of the Közraktár Street apartment house Mother lit our precious candles that she had recast over and over, placed them over a fir branch she found and spread three pieces of candy that Mary Kállay sent us via Trudi, who came often to see us. My parents stood silently a while, embracing. By way of a prayer, my father murmured his favorite line from a Hungarian operetta: "There will be yet grapes and soft bread." Then they blew out the candles, precious commodities that had to be saved.

Shortly after Christmas, the retreating Germans blew up all the bridges over the Danube and so we lost touch with Trudi. The bombing and cannon fire became constant and the house we were staying in was partially damaged with all of its windowpanes shattered. By December 31st everybody moved permanently to the cellar. People would only venture out to try to buy some food. One day they would get to the store running from doorway to doorway in between strafings, the next day they would find only a gaping hole in the place of the store and had to wonder whether the people who had served them were alive.

Retreating soldiers sold off their little stockpiles of food and my father managed to buy a bag of beans, hazelnuts, and a block of quince jelly, a stash that staved off starvation. When the house next door got a full hit, people ran out to collect the splintered wood of doors and furniture to feed a little stove in the cellar and keep from freezing in the bitterly cold winter. They dragged in usable furniture scavenged from the broken apartments. It was so that my parents gathered an armchair where Father slept and a sofa where Mother, Grandmami, and I slept for five weeks in the same clothes, covered by coats. Only one person had a kerosene lamp and oil. That was the only light source, sparingly used, for all day and night other than the precious candles people carefully recast. For a while we had running water in the cellar, but then it also gave out. My mother soaked overnight a handful of the dry beans that my father had bought, and pushed a few down my throat one by one in the morning to feed me. I was getting sick, with a fever and constant diarrhea.

People cooperated in the cellar. They were sorry for the sick baby and gave us some potatoes. Yet even in her desperation my mother couldn't help but think: "They are willing to help the refugees from Kassa. Would they share their food with the Jews? Or would they be glad that a Jewish baby was dying?"

The Soviets marched nearer every day. Hitler issued a command to resist until the end. About 100,000 German and Hungarian soldiers fought the Soviets street by street. On January 18th all of Pest, including the ghetto was liberated, with about 70,000 people, mostly children under sixteen and old people, still alive. But the Germans held Buda for another month in a last-ditch battle. The Russian soldiers commanded us to vacate the cellar so that they could use the remains of our apartment house, which was facing the Danube, as an artillery post to shell Buda. One family from the cellar found some relatives nearby and invited us to go with them for a few days. Then Mother found Lili, one of her Aryan friends, and we stayed with her for a bit. At almost ten months old I weighed the same as I had at four months and was too weak to lift my head. Just in time, Lili found a working Red Cross station that provided medicine and Ovaltine which seemed to help me. Keeping warm and staving off starvation continued to be the focus of our lives. Despite the continuous gunfire, people ventured out in search of firewood from broken furniture in the bombed-out houses and food—any food. One day, out searching, my mother saw a Russian soldier munching a piece of bread and noticed the crumbs falling on a low stone fence. After the soldier moved on, she kneeled down and licked the crumbs off the stone.

Slowly we found our family. Trudi found Miklós, very ill with a bleeding stomach or intestines (they didn't have the means to find out which), in the ghetto's makeshift hospital. She took him home to nurse. As soon as it was possible, my father went in search of news of his two grown daughters. Márta was just twenty-four when it was all over. She had been taken from the safe house toward the train to the camps but somehow escaped. Taken again, she managed to escape before the transport left Budapest. How or at what price she had escaped she was never willing to talk about.

Eva and little Gábor had found a place to hide, I don't know exactly where. Willie, Eva's husband managed to escape from a forced labor camp as things were falling apart, and find his way back to his wife and child two weeks before the liberation of Pest. But someone had ratted on them, and Eva and her little family were found. The Arrow Cross thugs came. Rather than taking them all away—God knows why—they wanted to take just Willie. Eva begged them to leave him. One of them replied, "Okay, we won't take him." With that he pulled out his pistol and shot Willie in the head as Eva stood next to him, holding their not quite two-year-old son. Eva has lived with that memory for over sixty years but could never speak about it without sobbing in a way that I knew she was not just remembering but reliving the moment. And we all have lived with the knowledge that she was turned away from Trudi's apartment by my father. It is irrelevant to argue whether or not we all would have been discovered and killed had we stayed together, but it is hard not to think about.

Except for Willie, our immediate family was intact. But when all the cousins, spouses, and children were accounted for, thirty-eight family members and many dear friends had been exterminated—not my word but the Nazis'—and not just by the Germans but also by their more than willing Hungarian followers. Yet we were luckier than Poland, Czechoslovakia, and Germany. One half of Budapest's 200,000 Jews survived though almost none did outside the capital. The Holocaust proper ended in April 1945. But my experience of it—and the experience of any other survivor—did not. As survivors trickled back to the city, as we started getting together with others, we heard the rumors confirmed. The nightmares of the cattle cars, of medical experiments, of the gold collected from the teeth before people were shoved into gas chambers, of soap being boiled out of the remains. My mother kept reliving in her imagination what happened to all of them as well as what happened to her. And talked about it—over and over and over again.

What she never talked about, and I am not sure ever thought about, was how all this could have happened. Only much later in life as the terror of it all receded, was I able to look at the Holocaust in Hungary and recognize that it wasn't just a sudden malignant eruption, but that it had understandable—though never justifiable—antecedents.

How Did We Get Here?

To search for the deepest antecedents of the Holocaust, for its historical context, I would need to look back centuries, even millenia. But I found that going back no farther than the second half of the nineteenth century provided me with a fair picture of what happened in Hungary.

My grandparents were born less than ten years after the establishment of a semi-independent Hungary in 1867. After a two-decade struggle for independence from Austria, a compromise created the Kingdom of Hungary alongside the Empire of Austria, forming the Austro-Hungarian Empire. Each kingdom had a sovereign government for domestic matters but a common one for foreign affairs.

In 1867, Hungary was a feudal agricultural society with several ranks of nobility, gentry, small landowners, landless peasants, and urban laborers. A society of the very rich and the very poor, with some small farmers and artisans, it had hardly any middle class. Once industrialization began in western Europe, however, many saw its promise.

Once again, as so many times before in history, Hungary found itself at the crossroads between East and West. Its eastern soul was steeped in a traditional land-based agricultural life; its western mind was ready to embrace a modern, industrial society. The gentry and the aristocracy, who were the only ones with any say-so in the future of the country were deeply divided. The lesser nobility and the gentry who lived on their land in ease and were the virtual rulers of life and death on their domain romanticized this life, viewing it as the tradition that imbued and formed the Hungarian soul. They despised entrepreneurship and commerce as something no real Hungarian would dirty his hands with.

On the other hand, many of the upper-echelon aristocrats (princes, dukes, margaves, counts) had been educated in the West and were taken with the philosophy of modernism and the industrial advances they had observed. They were enthusiastic anglophiles and francophiles. Although they owned the largest estates, they mostly lived in Budapest, where they held high positions in the government, and served on boards of banks and of large corporations. They envisioned Hungary becoming an important modern state within Europe, a significant industrial and commercial player. It was during those last decades of the nineteenth century that these super rich aristocrats built up Pest from a small commercial center on the other side of the Danube from Buda, to its present-day beauty of wide boulevards flanked by splendid neoclassic buildings.

The forward-looking leaders of Hungary had two major problems to solve before they could succeed. One was that modernization required a middle class, citizens who were professionals, entrepreneurs, and businessmen. The second was that Magyars (Hungarians), in order to gain undisputed power, needed to become a majority in the country. The Kingdom of Hungary, three times the size of Hungary today, contained many ethnic groups: Magyars, Germans, Czechs, Slovaks, Italians, Poles, Ukrainians, Jews, Romanians, Slovenes, Croatians, Serbs, and Gypsies. Magyars were but the largest minority, concentrated in the center of the country, a center that was ringed by mixed populations of Magyars and other ethnic groups. The other ethnic minorities were demanding increasing autonomy and resisting "Hungariasation." The solution to both the problem of needing a middle class and of becoming a majority was granting citizenship to the Jews and declaring them Magyars.

Thus Hungary followed the example of France and Germany, which very recently had offered the Jews citizenship if they were willing to swear allegiance to the country and consider themselves citizens of Jewish faith rather than Jews in Diaspora as they had for so many centuries. In 1895 Judaism was admitted among the legally recognized religions of Hungary and the seven percent of the population who were hitherto considered Jews were declared Magyars of Jewish faith. In that way Hungarians became the majority in the Kingdom of Hungary.

The liberal, urban nobility who wanted to see Hungary develop as a western society supported the complete civil and political equality of Jews. They no longer demanded conversion to Christianity, though they preferred it. They were looking for assimilation, for Hungarians who were talented and vested in industry, modernity, and progress. Nowhere in Europe were Jews more actively encouraged to assimilate and participate in the economic and civil life than in Budapest at the turn of the century. The Jews of Hungary responded eagerly, embracing the chance to become "real Hungarians." Most of them had always loved the country and longed to be truly a part of it.

The dream of belonging mostly succeeded for about three golden decades, to the end of World War I. In the last decades of the nineteenth century, Jews concentrated in Budapest and took advantage of their new opportunities, becoming twenty percent of the city's population by 1900. Traditionally intensely interested in education, by the turn of the century they accounted for almost half of business school and medical school students and over a quarter of law students. By 1910 almost half of the lawyers, doctors, and journalists, a third of the engineers, and a quarter of artists and writers of Hungary were Jewish. Many of these areas of study were new or recently expanded and of not much interest to the children of the landed gentry, who very much like their English counterparts, lived in a romantic dream of the perfect country life. The oldest son was lord over the land and its people, while younger sons occupied the leading positions in politics, the army, and the diplomatic core.

Jews—Hungarians of Jewish faith—became the educated middle class. They flourished as businessmen and professionals, especially in Budapest. A few families rose meteorically to the position of very wealthy industrialists, bankers, and financiers, heading huge concerns. They reached upper class status, and built villas, intermarried with rich Christians and some nobility, held literary and musical salons, and became society people. The mayor of Vienna referred to Budapest disdainfully, but not entirely unjustifiedly, as "Judapest."

But assimilation, or at least acceptance, turned out to be largely illusory. The concept of "other" persisted on both sides. Even those Christians who embraced the modern development of the country always were aware who was Jewish, even if they were willing to relate to them socially. Acceptance was never viewed as a natural human right, or as something merited, but something that was graciously granted to the Jews. A slightly strained note remained, a self-consciousness, that intruded upon the illusion. By and large, although Jews built a strong social life on a cosmopolitan model, patronized the arts, and took a leading part in the intellectual life of the city, they mostly interacted with each other. That was what felt comfortable and rewarding to them, and that was how they could avoid being conscious and leery of their Christian social equals.

The push and pull between modernity and tradition never abated. In 1900 Hungary celebrated the millennium of its founding, an opportunity for the gentry to further romanticize the national feudal past in opposition to the more rational and materialistic cosmopolitan modern life, which they viewed as corrupt and a betrayal of the Hungarian ideal. There was much discussion—novels, plays, newspaper articles, and general conversation—about the Magyar soul, the deep Magyar race, the Magyars of "good race." It became fashionable to dress in a stylized Hungarian folk costume and have faux Hungarian country furniture in the city. Literature idealizing the peasant and the country life grew in popularity. Many Hungarians viewed Budapest as divorced from the "real" Hungary, from the country where the soul of the nation resided.

The danger to their way of life that the feudal gentry saw in modernism was real. Modern agricultural methods and machinery introduced a different kind of cultivating, more capital intensive and less dependent on the peasants who belonged to the gentry and cost little. Peasants could go to the cities and work in industrial plants. The life of privilege and influence of the landed gentry was waning, and the more they lost, the more they clung to and glorified the past. Many who had to give up their farms found a place in the vast administrative network of national and local government, where they could speak for and act on their conservative views. Their children, who no longer had a viable farm to inherit, joined the army or drifted to Budapest to try to succeed in one of the hitherto despised professions. But once they arrived there, they found they had to compete with Jewish professionals for jobs as lawyers, journalists, architects, doctors, and engineers. In their eyes modernity and the Jews were conflated as the cause of their hardships. The perception spread among the Christian conservatives and the population in general that Hungarian national identity was racially threatened, and that the culture, politics, intellectual life, and society in general had to be purified to be saved.

Then through one fatal shot and the fatally stupid response to it, World War I erupted. Tied to Austria by a common foreign policy and the authority of Emperor Franz Joseph, Hungary had no choice about entering it.

But the consequences of losing the war were more disastrous for Hungary than for any of the other Central Powers (Austria, Bulgaria, Germany, and Turkey).

When the Allies (US, France, Great Britain, and others), made the losing Central Powers sign the Trianon Peace Treaty, they carved Hungary up and allocated large portions of it to surrounding nations who had joined the Allies. They simply gave Transylvania, with its two million Hungarians, to Rumania; united the Slovak region of Hungary, along with its huge ethnic Hungarian population, with the Czechs; and attached Slovenia and Croatia, which had been part of Hungary, to Serbia. Hungary lost to its neighbors two-thirds of its territories and population—all the areas that were ethnically mixed—together with more than two-thirds of its industries, prime materials, and financial institutions.

The nation was grief-stricken. Six hundred thousand Hungarians died in the war and now it lost several million more in a cruel and arbitrary peace treaty. The new, truncated Hungary had to figure out who it was. The country responded with a redoubled nationalism in what became known as "little Hungary" (as opposed to the "greater Hungary" of before). The ruling obsession of the Hungarian government and of the people deeply wounded in their national pride was the recovery of the lost territories. The slogan "little Hungary is no Hungary, greater Hungary is heavenly" echoed everywhere. News about mistreatment of and revenge on the Hungarians now belonging to the neighboring victorious countries fueled this obsession. The peace treaty was perceived as—and was—profoundly unjust. It led to widespread disillusionment with the League of Nations, the West, and the modernism it represented. Ultrapatriotic, conservative organizations sprung up all over the country. Even boy scouts and girl scouts were seriously trained for their mission of reclaiming the lost territories.

Anti-modernity sentiments and ideologies easily jelled around anti-Semitism. It all made a terrible sense: letting Jews into society was seen as an outcome of modernity that conspicuously benefited the Jews. The romanticized nationalism centered around a past that definitely did not include Jews as equals. It was based on the idea of a mythic, authentically Magyar race and nation, a concept very similar than was developing in Germany. This type of national identity required an "other," for contrast, and the image of the Jews as "the other," as they have been portrayed by Christianity for centuries, was readily available. The fact that all the areas with mixed population had been lost with the Trianon Peace Treaty played into this new type of nationalism, as Hungary found itself linguistically and culturally much more homogeneous within truncated "little Hungary." With that, one of the main reasons for inviting Jews to become Magyars had disappeared.

The country was in chaos. The Hungarian government owed huge war reparations to neighboring countries, industrial activity practically came to a standstill, and the agricultural market could not compete with western mass production. Both the government and the people fell into financial crisis. One third of the workforce became unemployed, creating poverty and hunger in the cities. Just when the formerly landowning gentry was forced to look for a place in the bureaucracy or the professions, the country, and with it the bureaucracy, shrank to less than half its size. Bureaucrats, army officers, and refugees of Hungarian ethnicity from the areas lost also poured into truncated Hungary looking for jobs, especially in commerce and in the professional fields. They found these jobs filled—many, though of course not all, by Jews. So Jews were blamed for the terrible economic situation.

Excluding Jews was the most obvious solution to opening up jobs and so the first anti-Jewish law (*numerus clausus*), restricting the number of Jewish university students was passed in 1920. Sadly for the country, the result was a large exodus of Jews, especially to the United States. Many of those Jews became well known scientists, artists, journalists in their new country (for example, physicists Leo Szilard, Eugene Wigner, Edward Teller, mathematician John von Neumann, chemist Albert Szent-Gyorgyi, economist John Harsanyi, filmmaker Alexander Korda, and photographer Andre Kertesz.) Several won Nobel Prizes in their fields.

The conflict between tradition and modernism continued to rage in the 1930s, splitting Hungarian literary and cultural life into populist and urbanist. Although there were many Christian liberal intellectuals, urbanists who were inspired by the development of Western democratic political thought, "urbanist" and "liberal" also became a populist code name to refer to Jews. It was the conservative populist faction that dominated political life, turning ever more to the right as the economic situation failed to improve. They formed the Hungarian Arrow Cross Party in 1935, following the line of Italian Fascism and German Nazism. Although almost every social group, from impoverished aristocrats to small industrialists and ex-military officers, was represented in the leadership of the party, the Arrow Cross especially gained popularity with the working classes in the most impoverished counties and urban districts.

The *numerus clausus* law didn't relieve anti-Jewish feeling in the country and the Arrow Cross loudly demanded more. The Ministry of Education responded by revising the school curricula at all levels to stress Christian and nationalistic ideologies. The minister declared that "the nation's political education can only be secured if it is permeated by Christian religious sentiment," and called for "re-Hungarianizing the nation's intellectuals in place of their Judaization." As the government and the population felt for the moment powerless against their triumphant neighbors they needed an enemy over whom they had some power and against whom they were able to vent their fury.

Party newspapers and literature encouraged anti-Semitism, reviling and caricaturizing the religious Jew but really targeting the assimilated Jewry, those who had benefited from modernization and emancipation. This group had become successful and could be accused of capitalism, of communism, of conspiring to rule the world—and more immediately and realistically—of blocking jobs and opportunities of their Christian brethren.

Hungarian society and the state had clearly abandoned the assimilationist social contract. But the Jewish intellectuals, like my father, couldn't afford to believe it and continued to be committed Hungarians, convinced that this wave of anti-Semitism was but a short, passing phenomenon. In an effort to affirm their Hungarian identity, Budapest's Jews republished in the newspaper the manifesto they published first in 1848, during the unsuccessful quest for independence from the Hapsburg Empire:

"We are Hungarians and not Jews, not a different nation, because we are a separate denomination ... but in every other aspect of life we are only patriots, only Hungarians."

They ended the republished statement with, *"We profess this even today, the spring of 1938."* This could be construed as a self-serving statement of a desperate people. It is the statement of a desperate people, desperate because even after seeing their dream disappear, they could not give up their love for the country, their longing to belong.

Yet they belonged less and less. The Anschluss, the attachment of Austria to Germany in March 1938, further encouraged the shift of the Hungarian government to the right. On May 28, 1938—my father's fiftieth birthday—the second anti-Jewish law was promulgated, limiting the percentage of Jews allowed in white collar professions, such as journalists, doctors, lawyers, and actors. The third law followed in May 1939, totally banning Jews from professional jobs. Ironically, the laws could not be fully implemented because there was a shortage of skilled labor and Jewish professionals and enterprises were vital to the national economy. But the *Nemzetör* ("National Guardian"), the ultra-nationalistic populist weekly started in 1938, continued to rail in its headlines against the "Judaization" of the professions, the Hungarian theater, the banking industry, and so forth, and kept calling for the enforcement of the law.

The *Nemzetör* was very effective in whipping up the population by instilling fear and by penning venom-saturated satire. Headlines warning that the Jews of Galicia (part of Ukraine) were taking over the northeast of Hungary, and that the Hungarian soil had to be cleaned from the Jewish plot of socialism, created fear. But satire was more insidious. For example, on the seemingly innocent topic of "spring is here":

> At night they frequent the bars, restaurants, theaters, movies. On Sunday morning the coreligionists start out in large groups for an excursion.... They take the tram, surging, jostling, loud. They can be recognized by hooked nose, jug ears, woolly curly hair, flat feet and strange sing-song speech. Their favorite topics: money, business, scary news. Their favorite food: goose liver.... Their knock-knees are visible from their wool socks ... on their feet are real leather shoes. Their loud shirts are visible from afar, in their buttonholes a Petöfi button [Hungarian hero, poet and freedom fighter of the 1848 uprising], a symbol to which they have no relation and the least right to display.... Their women ... have fashionable negro-brown faces, freshly tanned and powdered.... They return late afternoon, commenting "it has been a beautiful day."

The tram conductor agrees, but adds: "but what a beautiful day it will be when these disappear from Hungary once and for all." *Nemzetör*, 17 April 1942 (*translated by author*)

Probably no Jews read the *Nemzetör*, but if they did, what could they do? Some, like my mother's oldest sister and her husband, obtained visas to places that seemed safe, mostly the United States. But relatively few of those who tried to leave succeeded.

In September 1939, when Germany invaded Poland and in response Great Britain and France declared war on Germany, Hungary remained neutral. But the country was heavily dependent economically on Germany and Austria, who were its main trading partners. Hitler skillfully played on the principal obsession of Hungarians: regaining the territories lost in the Trianon Peace Treaty after World War I. Most of Hungary's actions in World War II were governed by this one goal.

Many in the Hungarian leadership, made up of old aristocrats, didn't care for the Jews. Horthy, the Regent, was a self-avowed anti-Semite. At the same time they considered themselves civilized men and expressed a profound distaste for the idea of a wholesale massacre. They also distrusted and disliked the rabid, emotional, plebeian Nazis and the Arrow Cross party. Therefore they were disinclined to embrace the Germans' war.

Although the governing nobility and intelligentsia were resistant and saw their mission as keeping Hungary sovereign and out of the control of Germany, the offer of regaining territories was a carrot they couldn't resist, especially given the popular sentiment on this issue. So Hitler slowly but inexorably drew the country into the war by "giving back" parts of Slovakia, as long as the Hungarian army provided the occupying troops. Hitler played Rumania and Hungary against each other, returning northern Transylvania to Hungary in September 1940. The euphoric jubilation in Hungary over regaining Transylvania went way beyond what this rationally could have meant to the people who did not live there. It wasn't just a territory but an idea, a vindication of a sense of self and of national greatness. The momentum was irresistible: in June 1941 Hungary officially entered World War II, joining the German invasion of the Soviet Union. Among the battalions sent to the Russian front were over 200 Jewish, unarmed, forced labor battalions. The loss of life in the general Hungarian army was tremendous. Of the Jewish unarmed battalions hardly any people survived.

Yet there was still no fighting on Hungarian soil, and life for most Hungarians continued with a sense of normalcy. The various newspapers published updates of the war every day, the tone running from neutral to warmongering and hate fueling, but everybody continued to read the ones that reflected their own stances. Most people were more concerned about internal politics and the economy, about the growing workers' movement and the illegal but active Communist Party. The war stimulated the economy and got the country out of the depression but at the same time created a shortage of food and other goods. The Jews, too, tried to live their lives, to weather the situation through. They hoped this was one more terrible period of persecution that would eventually pass. But the German demand that Hungary now cooperate in solving the Jewish Question became more and more insistent.

Regent Horthy appointed a new prime minister who was much more sympathetic to the Nazi cause, and in August 1941 the Parliament promulgated a new, sweeping anti-Jewish law "to defend the race." It prohibited marriage and sexual relations between Jews and Christians and for the first time defined Jewishness in racial terms. Anybody with two Jewish grandparents was considered Jewish. This

Jews lined up outside the Swiss legation hoping to obtain papers that would protect them from deportation. (Courtesy of the United States Holocaust Memorial Museum Photo Archives.)

included about 100,000 Christians of Jewish ancestry. The "*Nemzetör*" hailed the new law declaring that "a single drop of Jewish blood sufficed to spoil the character and patriotism of a person." Ironically, many of those ardent guardians of the Magyar race were not Magyars but minorities who lived in the country. Even more ironically, some of the leaders of the purifying movement were subsequently discovered to have Jewish blood. Confronted with the discovery, several killed themselves.

With utter illogic, Jews were blamed for the country's involvement in the war and the increasing shortages of food and goods. The frustration of the Christian middle class, industrial workers, and peasants was skillfully funneled away from the government and toward a scapegoat made ready by centuries of Christian religious teaching of the guilt of the Jews in Jesus' death. The increasing hate

Jews rounded up on the way to who knew where.
(German Holocaust archives)

propaganda, repulsive caricatures, and anti-Jewish laws, not just blaming but demeaning Jews to subhuman level, paved the way to society's acceptance of the deportation and massacre that followed.

But not quite yet. Horthy insisted that Hungary would retain its right as a sovereign state to resolve the Jewish Question independently; together with a few other outstanding Hungarian politicians he refused to be party to a massacre. How much their actions were motivated by simple humanity and how much by the fact that the war was not going well for the Germans is hard to tell. What is important is that Horthy's attitude bought time—and hence life—for Hungary's Jews.

Then on March 19, 1944, German forces invaded Hungary. The nightmare lasted almost exactly one year.

The year of our Holocaust was over in February 1945, with the liberation of Budapest. By April 4, 1945, all German troops were out of Hungary.

First Years

With the war and the danger over, Jews resurfaced in Budapest, straggling back from concentration camps and hiding places. They searched for their old homes and their families, and when relatives found each other, if one of them had a half-way habitable place, soon ten or twenty relatives and friends were living there.

My parents, too, were eager to return to what they hoped was still our apartment. We were in Pest, a very long way from the outskirts of Buda where we had lived. Because motorized transport was nonexistent except for military vehicles, everyone walked and so did we. Ours was a slow little procession: Grandmami, weak from pneumonia, her ample figure emaciated, my mother pulling me in a make-shift little wagon, my father carrying a bundle of the few things that somehow we still had. The streets were full of people trying to find their place, milling, gaping. We had to cross a temporary pontoon bridge over the Danube, all real bridges having been blown up by the retreating Germans. Large parts of both halves of the city, Buda and Pest, lay in ruins. The devastation was hardly possible to take in. Rubble everywhere. Big apartment houses half blown away, half intact, walls of apartments blown away yet with paintings still on the wall, displaying the insides like theater sets. Walls riddled with holes from machine gun and tank fire. Elevator shafts gaping, twisted iron wrecks.

The call went out, leaflets and megaphones, for people to help clear the rubble. People were eager to put the horrors behind, to rally to rebuild, to start anew, especially the young people, like my distant cousin Ancsa or my friend Alex's mother, Vera. As teenagers in the ghetto, they survived. In the months of yellow star houses and the ghetto, they and perhaps thousands of other young people shunned the present and dreamed of an ideal life. Their conviction that the younger generation, under communism, would create a good safe life for Jews, for the poor, for all, ran deep. They were ready to work hard and cleaning up the rubble felt like an appropriate start.

My parents were older, shell-shocked, less resilient, and disillusioned. They just wanted to go back to their old life. Our luck held. The building at Csévi Street 3 and the small apartment houses and villas around us were mostly intact and our thoroughly decent Christian neighbors had kept our things and returned them to us. Our condominium was on the top floor of a three-story house with two condominiums on each floor and a semi-basement concierge apartment. Mrs. Rónai and her widowed daughter, Claire, lived on the garden level apartment, two floors below us. My parents had given them the silver, some jewelry, and other precious things to keep safe for us and had asked them to keep an eye on our apartment. Someone must have moved into our place, probably a military officer, because they were the ones who occupied the nicer apartments of dispossessed owners or renters. Most people we knew who were able to return found their places ransacked and empty, but once again we were incredibly lucky: whoever moved into our place did not destroy or steal our furniture, and when they disappeared at the end of the war, we not only could return, but found many of our things in good condition.

One of the first things my father did when we returned was to plant a small English walnut tree in the garden as an affirmation of faith that we would be there long enough and safe enough to enjoy its fruits. So there was hope, but there was weariness and caution too. Most Jews lived with the question that they could never quite voice but that sat in the pit of their stomach when encountering a Christian: where were you in 1944? What did you do? Could you have been the man in that uniform who shot my brother or took my sister away?

My parents had learned their lesson; anyone who didn't know it already was not going to know that we were Jewish, ever again. The fact that there were very few Jews in our neighborhood and people didn't expect any made this resolution more realistic. In 1945 Father changed our family name from the German/Jewish "Fleischl" to the impeccably Hungarian sounding "Felhös," meaning "cloudy" (I never learned why that particular name was picked). I was too little yet to understand what the secrecy meant, but nevertheless could sense that we weren't quite right, quite like others, quite acceptable. The feeling that the world was an unsafe, threatening place, something I must have absorbed with my mother's milk in the first year of life, continued. And so we tried to make a new life.

My father managed to get the job of financial director of the National Theater in Pest. They didn't pay him much, but there was hardly anything to buy anyway. As part of the massive effort to try to normalize life in Budapest, the National Theater started functioning very early on, in 1945. Since no trams or buses could cross the one pontoon bridge connecting Buda and Pest and we lived so far, he lived for more than a year in Pest, sleeping in his office. For most of that time my mother walked three hours each way during the week to see him and take him clean clothes, and on Saturday mornings he walked the three hours across town to see us, returning Sunday the same way. A year after the end of the war they rebuilt the first bridge and public transport returned, and my father's visits became longer and easier. But up to almost my third birthday Father did not live with us and I hardly saw him.

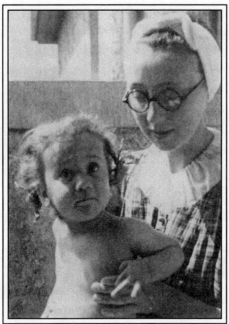

My mother and I in 1946
on the balcony of our apartment.

I didn't see much of my half-sisters either. They were off on their own, busy struggling to keep body and soul together. Eva had to take care of her little son and her mother-in-law, "Mutti" (diminutive for mother in German). After liberation Eva found Mutti and had to tell her how Willie was shot in front of her. At that point Mutti was still hoping that her other son, who was also taken to a forced labor camp, and her husband had survived. But they hadn't. Willie's father died in Bergen-Belsen and they were never able to find out what happened to Willie's brother. The three survivors, Mutti, Eva, and little Gábor, finally walked across the pontoon bridge like we did and made their way to the house at Ali Street, to the three-apartment villa that Willie's father had built for himself and his two sons.

Eva and Mutti found the house partially destroyed by a bomb. They managed to have one room repaired in the lower apartment by selling three cameras that they found in the rubble of their house. They found other precious family objects too, a crazy-making reminder of what life had been. Ali Street was in the beautiful Rosehill neighborhood of Buda, famous for its stately homes and lovely rose gardens. It was an isolated area; even in the best of times it had been a long bus ride into the city center, where most jobs were, and the buses weren't running yet into the outlying areas. Mutti and Gábor could stay there, but Eva had to find some place closer to the city center, where she could live and earn money. But how? She knew it was up to her to take care of herself and Mutti and Gábor. Our father could barely help her and she could not afford to despair. She could not afford to think "I don't know how."

Plucky and inventive, Eva had a bright idea. In the early months after the war there was no electricity in Buda yet, so all the cooking, heating, and work that could be done had to be done with charcoal, which was scarce. After overhearing a tailor complaining that he couldn't iron, she went to a bakery and asked them what they did with their used charcoal. They told her they threw it out, as it was no longer usable for baking bread. So she found a little wagon and went around to bakeries asking them for their half-burnt charcoal, and then went up and down the street garbed in her father-in-law's old shoes and shirt, blue from the cold, yelling "charcoal for sale." People bought this charcoal that could be still reused for lesser needs and gave her pennies for it, with which she could buy bread. She loved to tell the story later how at one house a woman leaned out the window and told her to come upstairs. When she did, the woman gave her a hot cup of tea and bread smeared with fat, a very rare treat then and manna for starving Eva. After she warmed up a bit the woman took her to her closet and gave her a pair of shoes and a warm dress. Eva could barely get a word of thanks out and burst into tears at the kindness amid the suffering. Later when things were better she went to thank the woman but she had moved. Eva never knew her name.

The charcoal enterprise brought in only pennies and it wasn't a long-term solution. Our father gave her a little money every month, but he could not support all of us. One relative suggested that Eva could get what was called a "trading permit" and use the connections she had from the past to act as a commercial agent. She had no idea how to do that, but she went to the old rubber factory where our father and Willie had worked to give it a try. The man who had been Willie's boss was eager to help. So now she had a job selling rubber parts to the heavy machinery factories. Why would they buy from her, when clearly she knew next to nothing of what she was trying to sell? Old family connections and solidarity within the web of friends saved her again, as they saved many people in those days. When the buyers found out what happened to her family, they were happy to order from her what they needed. Selling to Salgotarjáni Coal Co. and to Weiss Manfred's huge steel mill where her father-in-law had held a high position, Eva earned her agent's fee.

When she got paid she bought all the food she could find and afford, put it in a big rucksack, and walked the two and a half hours to Ali Street. Once there, she slept all weekend. Little Gábor couldn't understand why, when his mother was finally home with them, she wouldn't play with him. She was exhausted, physically weakened, with sores on her skin from malnutrition and sores on her feet from walking. Her nerves were shattered and she couldn't afford to look at the gaping wound in her heart, but was determined to survive and raise her son. Once again, her job didn't last long, because the coal companies and steel mills were among the first to be nationalized.

Gábor, her only grandson, gave Mutti a reason to continue living, and she also tried to help make ends meet. Her family owned the lot next door, which had been their orchard. Some of the trees that had not been split or cut down by the bombs and the debris started to bear fruit again. Mutti and Eva picked the fruit and tried to sell what they didn't put away for themselves or bring to us. When they could find and buy a little flour and sugar, Mutti baked cookies to sell.

Eva and sister Márta lived together for a while in 1946, subletting an unfurnished room, putting in a couple of mattresses and chairs they scrounged. Márta, having finished business school before the war, found a job in a large company's accounting department. In another apartment lived Andy Falus, a divorced man in his thirties. He met and fell in love with Eva, who even in her emaciated state was beautiful: tall, with shoulder-length blond hair, light brown eyes, a generous mouth and a ready laugh. Andy asked her to marry him. Barely a year and a half after the tragic loss of Willie, with whom she was wildly in love, she was indifferent to him, but the temptation to have his help, to make her life a little lighter, proved too much to resist. She agreed to marry him, much to the dismay of Mutti.

Andy did help. He found people to dismantle the top two floors of the house in Ali Street and use those materials to make the lower apartment habitable beyond just the one room where Mutti and Gábor lived. As transportation became easier, Andy and Eva could move in and Gábor had more time with his mother and also a father figure. Slowly more opportunities, food, and goods became generally available. Andy was devoted to Gábor and to Eva, and for a while life looked up.

Life started looking up for me too. My father came home to live. Sometime around my third birthday he finally left the National Theatre and was hired as a comptroller for a

My sister Eva with Gábor and new husband Andy,
with Mother and me in the garden of our apartment house.

manufacturing company, a job closer to his pre-war experience. We had it easier than my sister Eva and many, many other people. My father had skills that the struggling economy really needed, and our apartment and our furnishings had survived. He also took on several private clients for whom he acted as a CPA, some of whom must have been family friends, because there was an air of familiarity about their visits. I disliked when they came to the house, because I had to be very, very quiet and had no access to Father despite his being at home.

I was adored by my parents—although I know that more from my mother's diary and the stories that my grown half-sisters told me later, than from personal memories. At least, they loved the idea of me. In practice, however, they were tired, older, had seen their world crumble, and didn't quite know what to do with an energetic little one. But I know that they were amused by me. And no matter how much of a stern disciplinarian my father had been with Eva and Márta, by the time I was born he was 56 years old and had gone through all the suffering of the war, so he didn't have the heart, the energy, and perhaps the wish to provide such a stern upbringing. So, when not ignored, I was indulged, and in turn I adored my father.

"Watching for Papa" was a favorite game. Csévi Street started at the Pasaréti Square and went sharply upward. Ours was the second house and I could observe from upstairs, from the stairwell windows, when he would arrive on the bus. I would run wildly down the stairs and down the street to meet him and he would pick me up in his arms and carry me home. This little time was our only time together many a day. The byword, when he got home was always "Papa is very tired. You must be quiet."

Father had the big room of the apartment, which was generally off limits to me, making it ever so much more enticing. I can close my eyes and still see every detail. There was a big desk, made of dark wood, with a leather inset on the top, smooth to the touch. This was where he worked and saw clients. Sometimes I hid in the nook under the desk until he came in and he gave me a kiss before shooing me out. The glass-fronted bookcases that lined one wall filled me with wonder and it was one of my special rewards for being good to look at the books and pictures.

Father's bed was in that room too, with a large built-in

bookcase alongside it, partly filled with a long row of big black books, the Révai Encyclopedia. Close to his pillow hung a picture of my mother, younger and beautiful, that my father, who was an aficionado photographer, had taken when they were dating. Next to her picture hung a photo of my two half-sisters, blond Eva and dark haired Márta. "The Beggar Woman," a bronze sculpture made by Trudi of a woman, head bowed, covered by a shawl like Hungarian peasant women, sitting with her arms clasping her knees, had a place of honor on his night table. At night my father always put his wedding ring into the hollow of her lap. It was a special treat to be allowed to curl up on Father's bed with him and have him read me a story before going to sleep.

The balcony off his room, with its red and beige checkered floor, the brick-red metal table with curved white legs, and the white metal chairs, was another favorite spot. Some weekend mornings we would have breakfast there and my parents would speak in relaxed tones, and for a little bit all seemed well with the world.

But mostly it was not. Running the household was difficult for my mother and she was tense. She had to warm the water on the kitchen stove and haul buckets to the bathroom to bathe or the sink to wash clothes. There was a lot of washing to do with a small child. Her obsession with keeping things clean to protect me from germs made extra work as she waged war against city grime and with everything that might bring it into the house. Nobody had refrigerators so she, like others, had to shop most days, which included going far afield since there was enormous scarcity as well as rationing. This hard life was not what her upbringing as the talented, sensitive youngest daughter of a well-to-do family had prepared her for. She had no chance to heal from the trauma of the war, the hiding, the fleeing and fearing for her and her baby's life. She had to jump in and try to make ends meet, keep us fed and clean, and respond to the demands of a curious toddler's incessant questions and need for attention. She was thirty-nine years old and tired.

Grandmami never recovered fully from the pneumonia she developed during the days of bombing and living in the shelter with no means of keeping warm and was sick often. So she could keep an eye on her, my mother sublet a tiny apartment for her not far from us on the top floor of one of the many large homes that had been subdivided. We walked along Pasaréti Avenue to visit her a couple of times a week during that bright and sunny spring in 1948, past gardens with cosmos, pansies, and roses, Mother answering my incessant questions, naming the flowers, explaining why they die, and how spring would turn one day to winter, but then spring would come again.

Grandmami was round and soft, wore black, and smelled fragrant. I knew she loved me and I loved to curl up in her lap. She had her own pet name for me, "Tuturchek Süssinko," a further diminutive of Tücsök (Cricket), my parents' nickname for me. My mother and Grandmami always spoke with each other in German, which I understood just as easily as Hungarian. My father and mother went back and forth between Hungarian and German until 1948, when my father thought it would be politic to speak only Hungarian. Then he insisted that I only speak Hungarian, though my mother liked my speaking German when he was out of earshot.

My grandmother, who had grown up in Vienna and had only moved because of my grandfather's work, lived thirty-four years in Hungary without ever quite learning the language. The family never stopped viewing their stay in Hungary as temporary and thinking of Vienna as their home. In a way, they got suspended in time and never settled. Speaking German in Hungary wasn't unusual, since it had been the language of the Austro-Hungarian Empire that all educated people spoke fluently. After the war it wasn't popular to speak German, but my mother never became really comfortable with Hungarian and retained a slight accent, even though she lived in Budapest from age seven to age fifty.

My father, on the other hand, loved the country and its language and literature. One of the few treasurers that I have from him is a hand-notated, leather-bound volume of a wonderful philosophical play, "The Tragedy of Man," written by Imre Madách, a playwright and poet who, like many of Hungary's well-known literary figures, also took part in the 1848 revolution. I remember overhearing Father argue politics with Mother, who was anything but a patriotic Hungarian, and can still hear the wistful love and hurt in his voice. Only many years later did I grasp his pain that his country had, in essence, rejected him and tried to kill him.

Juszti néni (néni or aunt, didn't only refer to a relative but was the honorific by which young people addressed older women), my parents' pre-war housekeeper who had given us her niece's birth certificate when we hid with false identities as refugees from Kassa, reappeared in our lives. She came back to help with the hard daily grind of cleaning, shopping, and cooking, allowing my mother a little more time to spend with me and to care for her own mother. Juszti néni may have been a godsend for my mother, but I feared her large bosom, booming voice, and flowing white hair. She had brought up a few children herself and brooked no nonsense from me. Our battles were often around eating, which interested me little. Food was very scarce and everybody was hungry, so beyond worrying about my health, the idea of wasting any food must have galled them. Mother would cajole me or threaten me with imaginary bogey men so I would eat or be quiet but Juszti néni's piercing look at me was sufficient.

In the fall of 1947 my Aunt Ruza came to visit from Belgrade. She was my father's second cousin, but because her branch of the family had moved to Serbia, they didn't know each other as children. The story of how they met seemed like a fairy tale to me. My father was an army officer in World War I. (In Franz Joseph's army all ethnic groups were integrated, so despite being Jewish, this was possible). His unit marched into a Serbian town as the occupying force, and as an officer he was to be housed there at the local lawyer's home. As he entered the home, embarrassed because of the system of forcing themselves on the local population bothered him, he was shocked to come face to face with a portrait of his paternal grandparents hanging on the wall. The local lawyer turned out to be his cousin Ruza, the first female lawyer in Serbia!

Despite this story, Aunt Ruza seemed to me a forbidding presence. Being the daughter of my father's aunt, she had been brought up with the same stern, unbending discipline as my father, which was meant to toughen you up for life. But unlike my father, she hadn't yet softened. I was even more afraid of her than of Juszti néni.

Taking advantage of the fact that Aunt Ruza was there as well as Juszti néni, my parents, worn out and having had no chance to really sit back and catch their breath since the nightmare of 1944, decided to travel to Bosnia, to see Bled, Sarajevo, and Mostar, places that they had loved to visit before the war and that held sweet memories for them. I didn't understand their need. I felt abandoned and betrayed, as well as scared and indignant, and their leaving me like that reinforced in my three-year-old self that there was nothing to trust in this world. One of my most vivid memories is having to lie down to take a nap, not something I was used to. There was a tall tree outside the window and its branches, moving with the wind, created shadow patterns on the ceiling that I knew were monsters, reaching out for me, closing in on me. I was scared out of my wits but when I cried and screamed I was sternly scolded and then ignored. It was a long two weeks.

I was jumping wild, excited, when my parents came back and Aunt Ruza left, but was quickly quieted down. My father was ill. Although my parents didn't know it then, it was the beginning of bleeding, cancerous colitis, a three-year ordeal that ended in his death. Even ill, Father kept on with his daily routine, including playing tennis or fencing before work every morning. He loved physical exercise or at least was a great believer in it for health reasons. He continued to be a rare and treasured presence in my life, the most beautiful man. He was tall, not only from my small vantage point but actually six feet, which for someone born in 1888 was considered quite tall. He had a tickling black mustache, high cheekbones and dark brown eyes that twinkled when he looked at me, even when tired and in pain.

My father's illness became a constant presence, a dark cloud of quietness. Eva's new troubles brought a spike of excitement into it. Budapest in 1947 was full of wheeling and dealing, as the city and the people tried to recover from the war, clear up the ruins, repair the buildings, and start up commerce again. Eva's new husband, Andy, got involved in some speculative deals that did not pan out and got himself deep in debt. He always looked for the next deal to solve all their problems, and so wanted Eva to put up the Ali Street house as security for a new venture. Although Willie's father had put the house in all their names and she and Mutti were the only survivors, Eva did not feel it belonged to her. And even if it did, she was not willing to jeopardize the roof over their head. She said no.

Andy became crazed. He threatened her with a pistol and told her he was going to kill her. That night he confessed that he had already forged her name to the promissory note using the house as security for his latest venture and that it was coming due and he couldn't pay it. Then he solemnly told her, "Tonight is the night you are going to die." Mutti and Gábor slept in the next room with no clue about what was happening. Eva was terrified and had the strength that terror and necessity lends us. She pretended to be asleep and finally, emotionally exhausted Andy fell asleep. She got up quietly and in the middle of the freezing night (it was January 1948) walked the half-hour to our place.

In the morning, Andy figured that our house was the place Eva would have gone. He came. Father let him in. Being a man of reason and considered decisions, he didn't imagine that his son-in-law had a pistol on him. He left Andy and Eva alone and the three of us sat quietly in the other room. Andy begged Eva to return with him and when she refused, he threatened her with the pistol again. A scream pierced the air and my parents ran into the room, pushing me back as Andy ran out the door and shot himself through the heart in the little landing between the two apartments. I shrank as a big bang echoed in the stairwell. The bullet went through him and through the door of our neighbor's apartment. Thankfully, our neighbors were not in their foyer at the time. But I saw the little square of lighter wood that patched their door every time I came and went.

What Eva must have felt, how the noise of that shot must have echoed the shot that a bare two-and-a-half years before had killed Willie, I can only imagine. She suffered a nervous breakdown and was placed in a mental hospital on a sleep cure for a couple of weeks. My mother surely must have felt terribly sorry for her but she was also ruthless in defense of her own cub. Her indignant tirades that Andy could have killed me by accident still reverberate.

When Eva could work again, she found a job in a department store selling sweaters. Eva didn't put on airs; treating people as people was part of her upbringing and being sociable and outgoing was part of her nature, both of which held her in good stead since Hungary was entering an era where equality was stressed and any kind of privileged background made you a despised pariah. She ate her bread and mustard or bread and fat and gossiped with the other sales women. One day a customer recognized her, exclaiming: "But dear lady, aren't you Mrs. Holzmann? Didn't I used to bring you clothes to try on from the Salon Denes?" Eva had to admit it. The woman went on and on about how much she liked to go to Eva's house, because Eva would talk to her and was so considerate. After a moment she asked, looking around, "But what happened to you?" Then, understanding dawning in her face, "Oh, you are Jewish…." Eva had to agree again.

When the woman left, Eva wondered how the others would relate to her now. They all had heard the woman's loud comments. She was afraid of nastiness and petty retaliation when they found out she wasn't "one of them," that she didn't have a working-class background. But if anything, she was treated with a little extra kindness and some admiration by the others because she was willing to work as hard as anyone. Although I was only four, I remember Eva sitting in the brown chair in our father's room, telling us the story.

Around that time Grandmami fell ill with pneumonia again and was in very bad shape. Mother insisted on bringing her to our apartment so she could care for her properly. Her sister Trudi was taking care of her sick husband, Miklós, who could not get healthy after his ghetto experience. Mother was also taking care of a sick husband and on top of it had a small child. In any case, my mother adored her mother and having mastered early the role of "dutiful daughter," she thought it was up to her. So, over my father's opposition, she brought Grandmami home and we, three generations of women, slept in the one room. I thought it was great because keeping company with Grandmami was fun; she would play with me as she was lying there, propped up on pillows in the big bed and never had a cross word.

Mother must have been squeezed between taking care of both Grandmami and my father and having a small child who demanded attention. There were in those days no children's records, not even children's radio programs, and only very few children's books. I played by myself, with my beloved teddy bear that my father had given me when he was still working in the theater. My imaginary playmate, Anna, was also a good companion—up to a point. Playing in the garden with Anti Réfi, the son of our kind concierge family who was also four, was more satisfying but also more frustrating. While Anna always did what I wanted, Anti was bossy.

I guess I desperately wanted some of my poor, tired mother's attention and one way to get it was misbehaving. One night when I was in the bathtub I refused to get out when she told me to. Losing her patience, she hauled me out yanking my arm and told me: "Listen, in this household, first comes Father. Then comes Mother. Then for a very, very long time, comes nobody. And then comes little insignificant you!" She didn't know what this message would become for me. For a long time she had been fighting a heroic battle of survival and of making things all right. But that message was seared into me.

At the end of June 1948, about two months after she had come to stay with us, Grandmami died. When my parents knew that death was imminent, they sent me to stay with a friend down the street. I was sad and angry when I was told that she had died, feeling that if I could have given her one more kiss, that would have made it all right. Mother explained that I would see her in heaven, but that did not do much to salve the ache of her being gone. Every night as I kneeled to pray, I would pray for her in heaven, trying to imagine what heaven was.

Despite all she had suffered for being Jewish, mostly at the hands of Catholics, my mother retained and taught me her Catholic faith. She taught me about a loving God who forgave all and who loved all. She struggled to include Hitler in that, but she couldn't quite and I remember her outbursts about Hitler having to be in hell despite an all loving God.

We went to Mass practically across the street from us at the big church dedicated to Saint Anthony that dominated Pasaréti Square. At the center of the square, on top of a white column there was a lovely slender bronze statue of the Virgin Mary holding baby Jesus. A round garden of flowers surrounded it. At the entrance to the church there was a statue of St. Anthony, where I would kneel to pray. At age four or five I didn't understand the theological niceties but I did absorb a faith in a loving Father who will eventually make right all pain and injustice. So I loved my evening prayers, which were conversations with this wonderful, powerful being, and I didn't hesitate to ask for my earache to go away, or, regularly, for Father's health. And now I prayed for Grandmami in heaven, which was a good place but didn't allow visits.

After the upheaval with Eva's husband Andy and Grandmami's death in June, Father was weakened by continuing bouts of bleeding. My parents decided that a little time away would do us all a world of good. We went on a four-day vacation to the village of Bükszentkereszt, not that far away but definitely country. I think it was my first train ride. We stayed in a little inn with very good food and goats and chickens around, a new and exciting world. The country smell of that place still fills my nostrils.

One of my sweetest childhood memories is from that vacation. We are walking up a dirt road at dusk, Mother holding my one hand and Father the other. For a bit I had the sense that all was well with the world and I have cherished that moment all my life. But the sense of life's precariousness that started at birth or earlier kept cropping up. Even during our little vacation Father's illness became worse.

Yet there were days, even weeks, when he was feeling better and everything seemed lighter. I remember even an evening when my parents decided to go to the theater. I was left with Juszti néni, which made me unhappy. But what I most remember is when my parents said good night. I looked at my mother maybe for the first time and saw not just my mother but a separate person. In her deep purple suit, she looked lovely. Slender, almost totally white haired (it had turned that way during the war), long-necked, she reminded me of a picture of a gazelle in the Révai Encyclopedia. She moved like I imagined a gazelle would. Her green eyes shone happy that night and her face was relaxed.

Father's cousin, Aunt Ruza, reappeared in our lives in the summer of 1948. The Yugoslav Prime Minister, Tito, was trying to break free from the Soviet Union and try his own brand of socialism. The country was in turmoil and it was not clear how the power struggle would end. Aunt Ruza decided to flee Belgrade with her two daughters, Ivanka in her early thirties and Vera in her late twenties. Since in Hungary the situation was still more open, her idea was to go west through Hungary and eventually emigrate to Venezuela, where she had some friends. But the relations between Hungary and Yugoslavia were very tense and the border was well patrolled. They got caught by the Hungarian side. Fortunately they were allowed to call my father, who took the long train ride south and appealed to the patriotism of the border patrol officers and their resentment for having lost part of Hungary to Yugoslavia after World War I. He convinced them that since these women were his relatives they were really Hungarian, part of the old, big Hungary, the "real" Hungary.

Aunt Ruza and her daughters lived with us for about two months until they got papers in order to emigrate. With my parents there and me a year older, she seemed less forbidding, and I liked Vera very much. Having all the commotion in the house was also fun. Father slept with us, giving his room over to Aunt Ruza and her daughters. Somehow Father's illness was less in the foreground and my mother, who liked Aunt Ruza and the girls, seemed lighter. Eventually they left, my father lending them some money to get started. Little did he know that that money would help my mother and me get started in Venezuela nine years later.

Growth and Loss

In 1949 the Communist Party, puppet of the Soviets, took over in earnest and life became again progressively more difficult and more precarious.

At the time though, we were mostly occupied with the precariousness of our little family. My father's health was growing considerably worse as he bled from the rectum almost constantly, becoming weaker and weaker and most of the time in pain. Medical care in Hungary at the time was poor and equipment and medicines were scarce. I understood that my mother was sick with worry, but what I experienced was that she was short-tempered and unreachable. When my parents closeted themselves in the bathroom, I felt frightened and wanted to know what they were doing. So I climbed up the chair and tried to look into the bathroom through the frosted glass insert on top. Mother caught me and was livid with fury. Her contorted face turned beet red and I could have sworn that sparks flew out of her green eyes as she yelled at me. Then I felt even more frightened and excluded.

So I acted up. I wouldn't be quiet, I would nag for attention, and especially I wouldn't go to sleep. Mother often threatened that my toys (and I had but a few) would disappear from the shelf if I didn't shape up. One night when I had been "bad," after I went to sleep my parents decided that in order to maintain credibility they had to hide them. When I woke up, I turned to the shelf, eager for a new day, and saw the toys were gone. I was quiet a while, feeling something tender inside me leave and a hardness come in. "I guess I'll have to learn to live without toys," I said. My mother told the story later, saying how impressed and confused she was that I didn't cry and didn't promise to be good. Impressing her was not my purpose. I distinctly remember seeing the empty shelf and feeling a giant emptiness.

That morning something changed me. I could not have articulated it then, but somehow I understood that if I didn't want things (or people, or love), those things wouldn't have power over me, and I wouldn't get hurt. I learned that not letting anyone or anything too close might protect me from hurt. In some way that understanding has been helpful. I tasted the sense of power that detachment can bring but lacking the wisdom necessary I misinterpreted it. And, of course, it didn't really work, at least not always, for I longed for love plenty and got hurt plenty. But I never cared much about those toys or other things again, and that proved to be very helpful later on as we moved from continent to continent leaving each time most of our possessions behind.

Despite the atmosphere filled with tension all around me with my father's illness, I was still a five-year-old, craving play and laughter—craving normalcy. Play and laughter often accompanied Eva and Gábor's visits. I was very proud of and awed by my nephew who, ten months older, was tall and seemed like a gentle giant. Eva, despite all her tragedies loved to play as my mother never did and she would go down on all fours to give us rides around the room hee-hawing. Other times I played with the Réfi children, Anti, and his sister, Marika. Two years younger, she made a perfect baby for playing house. She looked like a beautiful doll, with blond curls and blue eyes and a sweet disposition.

The garden of the house was long, separated from Csévi Street by a fence and separated on the other side by a row of lilac bushes and olive trees. No real olive tree could grow in Budapest, but that's what they were called and they had a wonderful fragrance that wafted up in the summer through the open window of our third floor apartment. They also had fuzzy little "fruits" that we loved to eat. The old lilac bushes not only smelled wonderful but with their sturdy bare lower branches provided a great opportunity for building tunnels and hiding places among the bushes. Anti and I arranged a spot perfect for playing house at the lower end of the garden, which also became our convenient shortcut to Pasaréti Square.

Climbing sorrel, delicious to chew on, covered the iron mesh fence on the Csévi Street side. Around the entrance to the house the fence was different, built with a low stone ledge and stone pillars with horizontal iron bars between the pillars. We used those bars for our gymnastics, inventing all kinds of moves for our agile and graceful young bodies.

But these were only distractions. The center was held by my father, whom I adored, about whom I worried, who was my north star. He carried a sadness and remoteness that I wanted to breach, but his gravitas also offered a welcome counterpoint to my mother's volatility and unpredictability. When Father felt better the mood in the house lifted. On one of those good days my mother insisted that we go to the garden and took a picture of Father and me. I cherished that picture after he died, taking solace in his loving look. Only once do I recall my father being less than indulgent to me. He happened to look out of the window and see me running on the street, racing up the hill next to a delivery truck. As I walked in from the stairway into the foyer of our apartment he emerged from the dining room, his voice mad but calm. He explained the danger I put myself into and then gave me a spanking. I felt that that was fair.

As a toddler, I would put on my father's big, black-framed

One of the rare photos with my father, 1947.

glasses and pretend to read. By five I was reading and counting, and learned early that intellectual accomplishments were highly valued in my family. I spent many hours poring over the pictures in the multi-volume encyclopedia we had, and though other times my mother would shoo me away, she always tried to answer my encyclopedia questions and rewarded my observations with laughing delight and retelling to Aunt Trudi and to friends.

Public schools in Hungary did not have kindergarten then, but I went to a private kindergarten across the street, in what before the war had been a monastery attached to our church. Being in a group and having new playmates and just getting away from home was exhilarating. Kindergarten offered other delights too: It was there that I had my first banana, hardly seen in Hungary then. The US Consul, whose daughter was in the kindergarten, sent them for all the children. It was beautiful, yellow and firm, and I can still remember the sensuous feeling of opening and tasting it.

The home of the US Consul and his family was directly opposite our apartment house, a big old home with ivy covered walls, venerable looking, set back from the fence by a large garden. The family included my lovely new classmate, a mischievous pigtailed girl, infinitely more worldly than me, who invited me occasionally to play. It was she who introduced me to chewing gum, nonexistent in Hungary, a mysterious and scary treat, as she regaled me with stories of how it would turn into a stone in my stomach if I swallowed it by mistake.

For Father's birthday, May 28th, Eva, Márta, and Gábor

always came for dinner. His 61st birthday, in 1949, was a big deal not only because my mother and grown-up sisters understood how ill he was, but also because food was scarce, scarcer than it had been the two years before. Meat, eggs, and butter were hard to come by and very expensive. Ordinarily we ate cumin soup (a roux made with lard and added cumin seeds, dissolved with a bunch of water), legumes (with luck cooked with a pork bone), and potatoes and onions cooked with lard and paprika. An egg was a big treat, and dark bread (the only kind we had) with lard, a favorite.

For that special day my mother went on a hunt and hoarded the birthday ingredients days ahead, difficult because nobody had a refrigerator. We did have an icebox and in the summer the horse-drawn wagon came selling ice, but May was too early for the iceman.

I remember "helping" my mother in the kitchen that day, the cake she made, the fresh green pea soup. Finally it was dinner time. We gathered in the dining room, paneled in smooth blond wood with darker stripes, at the long table and sat on the chairs with woven straw-like seats matching the paneling. Even without the colorful painted ornamentation of real Hungarian folk furniture it all had a Hungarian feeling. It was a wonderful evening. Eva and Márta told stories about when they were young, teasing Father about how strict he had been with them and how spoiled I was, everyone laughing. We felt like a real family, large and together, as we savored our cheesecake.

My sister Márta was the rebel whom everyone loved in an indulgent, bemused kind of way. Much shorter than

Eva, she had short wiry dark hair and large brown eyes that reminded me of the pictures of Bambi in my book. She had no time for pretty dresses or lipstick. She liked sports, especially kayaking and camping, and she insisted on riding her motorcycle everywhere. Her whole demeanor was eager, slightly leaning forward. She learned or inherited from our father a stiff-necked application of principles regardless of the consequences to herself or others. She suffered the consequences of her principled actions with such idealism, always expecting the best of people, that it was hard not to admire her even as we watched her get hurt.

She worked in the bookkeeping division of Electroimpex, a large electric and electronic manufacturer that became nationalized in 1948 along with all other large concerns. The companies held hour-long educational events every morning before work began, such as reading aloud from the newspapers or communist tracts. The events were ostensibly voluntary, but those who failed to participate were ostracized, considered bad worker material, and passed over for promotion. After Eva convinced Márta that not attending these sessions was sheer stupidity, she finally went one day. When the name of Stalin, or Rákosi (Hungarian Prime Minister and Head of the Communist Party) was mentioned in an article or a speech, everyone was supposed to stand up and applaud. So everyone did—except Márta. To nobody's surprise but hers, she was promptly fired. A coworker named Balassa, impressed by her gumption, went out of his way to find her and sympathize with her. He became Márta's on-again off-again love and friend until his death some forty years later.

Márta next went to work as a bookkeeper in a factory, a rough place but where she could be more independent, and was allowed to wear slacks and ride her motorcycle. I admired my daring big sister very much. She was such a contrast to my mother, who was always afraid, always trying to protect me and keep me clean. Although Márta was twenty-three years older than I, she felt like a true sister, who never condescended but took me seriously and clearly loved me. I often begged her to take me for a ride on her motorcycle and once she relented. Holding on to her tightly I felt like we were flying, as the air caressed me and my hair was streaming behind me. I didn't want it to ever end. Somebody must have seen us and told my mother who was furious at poor Márta, so that was my only ride.

The department store chain where my sister Eva worked also was nationalized in 1949. But she was kept on, working for the new directors. The major—if not the only—requirement for the new management under communism was that they all had to be working class and party members. Often these managers were intelligent, well-meaning people, but simply not prepared by background or education for the jobs they were given and sometimes they had the grace and self-assurance to admit it. One Sunday when Eva came to visit she told us the story laughingly but admiringly about her boss. The company was trying to develop commercial relations with the West and a couple of British businessmen arrived for meetings. One of the directors summoned Eva and said, "I know that you are supposed to offer coffee to the visitors and that there is a special way of serving it. I don't know what it is. Will you serve the coffee? I am sure you know the proper way." Eva was touched by the woman's honesty and not only did the honors with the coffee but diplomatically tried to clue her in on other occasions as well. Yet soon, over the director's protest, Eva had to be demoted to sales secretary because her background was not sufficiently proletarian.

Ironically, the very stress and insistence about a proletarian background kept the class system alive and well and in everybody's mind. Perhaps it kept those of peasant or working class background triumphant as well as resentful and feeling less than prepared. I know it left me and mine aware that we had had a privileged position, that education and a background of culture and sophistication made us somehow better even if we were now punished for it. Even at six-years old, as I listened to the conversation of adults around me, heard Eva's amused story, this is what I understood.

What Eva earned in that job could not support her plus Gábor and Mutti. Every evening, after her job at the department store ended, she went to work as a typist for a lawyer until 9:00 in the evening. When even that wasn't sufficient, Mutti had to sell the once beautiful house, now mostly a ruin, and the orchard next to it in exchange for a two-room apartment and a year's worth of coal so they wouldn't freeze. With her long work hours, Eva couldn't live in Rosehill and had to find another place nearer the city center.

She found a room with her cousin Agi, whose family was also murdered. There one night she met Agi's friend, Endre Kálmán. He was a commercial attaché who had just returned from the consulate in Moscow and was being sent to Belgrade. Endre was very taken with this tall blonde who loved to laugh. She was not particularly attracted to him but found him amusing and intelligent, though she couldn't understand his deep and serious allegiance to communism. When he asked her to marry him and go with him to Belgrade, she refused. From abroad he wooed her with witty, interesting letters and weekly phone calls. As Tito successfully broke with the Soviet bloc, relations between Yugoslavia and Hungary became inimical at the directive of the Soviets, and Kálmán (she always called him by his last name) was recalled from Belgrade. When he got back to Budapest, he asked Eva again to marry him and asked her to choose which of the three foreign postings open to him he should accept next. She couldn't resist the prospect of living abroad and having an easier life with someone who was interesting and attentive, so even though she wasn't in love with him, she accepted and chose Italy.

In the end the Foreign Ministry did not allow Eva to go with her new husband. She wasn't a member of the Communist Party and her background wasn't working class, a definite requirement by 1950 that Kálmán couldn't overcome even with his considerable influence. He went on his posting and found a girlfriend and did the same with subsequent postings. The marriage became mostly in name only and eventually ended in divorce. Eva had to go back to work at the department store as a typist in the sales department.

In early 1950 we all started to be affected by the political situation, as wholesale deportations from Budapest started. The government or the Communist Party—the distinction was very blurry—consigned military officers from the war, nobility, prewar owners of medium to large shops or factories, and intelligensia who were suspected of not being faithful communists to the barren countryside, regardless of age or infirmity. There they were left to their own devices or made to work in the fields and cooperatives. They were not allowed to return to the city. Everyone had to carry personal identification which included addresses, and had to have permits to be outside their region of residence and work, so this was easy to enforce. In addition to being a punishment, the government used deportation as a way to ease a little the housing shortage in Budapest.

Our family was not immune from the fear of deportation, my parents were university educated people, my mother the daughter of a banker, and my father an ex-financial officer of a large industrial concern. We fit the profile. The police came Monday, Wednesday, Friday mornings before 9:00 to notify those to be deported, giving them twenty-four hours to arrange their affairs and get together the one piece of hand-luggage that they were allowed to bring along. Then on Tuesday, Thursday, and Saturday trucks with special police came to escort them away. For the deportees who were Jewish this was eerily reminiscent of Nazi deportations a mere six years before. We heard horror stories of those deported starving or freezing to death. My mother's already strained nerves became worse and I tried to stay out of her way as she exploded, "I can't go through this! Sándor [my father's name in Hungarian] wouldn't survive a week! What will we do? Should we leave the child with Juszti if we have to go?" I wanted to scream, "What do you mean, leave me?" but I didn't dare.

Mother's terror seeped into my uncomprehending mind as she would peek down the kitchen window watching for the gray car of the AVO (the Hungarian KGB, euphemistically called "Organization for the Protection of the Nation"). One day they stopped in front of our building. My mother and I were watching and I could feel her tremble as she held me. But the gray-uniformed men didn't reach the third floor. They came for Mr. Seléndi, Uncle Bandi, who had served in the old Hungarian army. A kind man, he was over 50, with a game leg. He and his wife, Aunt Ilonka, lived on the first floor and were good friends of my parents, and I loved them. We watched in mute despair the next day as they were taken away. They were permitted to return to Budapest about four years later, now two very old and broken people. They weren't allowed to return to their apartment, because part of the whole deportation game was to give apartments to the "worthy" servants of the state. Uncle Bandi died shortly after.

The Seléndi's apartment was given to an AVO lieutenant named Tóth and his family. The cozy camaraderie of the seven families felt threatened and we had to be very careful about what could be overheard in the building. Mr. Tóth was seldom there and sensing that we were afraid of them, the family kept to themselves. Polite reserve was maintained on both sides.

When 9:00 am passed on a Monday, Wednesday or Friday, we were safe for another forty-eight hours and there was a palpable letting go in Mother. The deportations were like Russian roulette. My mother's mystical side often verged into the superstitious: she gave up smoking, saying that as long as she didn't touch a cigarette, we wouldn't be deported. Our number didn't come up, and she never smoked again.

The food situation that had been slowly improving as the war years receded deteriorated as the communist regime rose, and we often went hungry. There were ration cards for everything. Father continued to get worse and weaker, going in and out of the hospital the first half of 1950, then mostly in. The hospital was in Pest and it took a long time on the bus to visit every other day. In food-poor Budapest the hospitals could only serve thin soups and legumes, so my mother redoubled her scrounging and borrowing and carried treats, a cooked egg, rice cooked in milk, or a little piece of chicken to the hospital to feed my father. Sometimes she begged Trudi for a bit of veal. Trudi's husband, Miklós, had special medical prescription that allowed for a priority ration of veal or chicken because of his stomach ulcers that hadn't healed since 1944. So sometimes they would share and let Father have a bit. It is difficult to fathom today—either in America or in Hungary—how large a sacrifice this was.

Almost as a talisman of hope for Father's recovery, Mother started to put together an album for their eleventh wedding anniversary, gathering photos from when they first started dating and from their years together. Every evening she sat at the desk sorting the photos, gluing in the photo corners, putting in the pictures and souvenirs, writing the history of their lives around the photos. I sat next to her as

My mother correcting my father's English paper.
Photo taken around their wedding in 1939.

My father in 1939.

she showed me the pictures and told me the story of their life together as she wrote it. I listened hungrily.

After her father had lost most of his fortune in 1931 the life Mother knew up to then ended. To support herself she put to use the degree she just earned from Oxford and started to teach English privately in 1932. One of her students was Eva Fleischl. When Eva's father wanted to brush up on his English, Eva recommended her as a teacher. And so my mother, twenty-seven-year-old Marianne Donner, and my father, forty-five-year-old Alexander Fleischl, met in the fall of 1933.

My father came for his English lessons on Sunday mornings, the only time he had available. In the spring he proposed that they take a walk in the beautiful Buda hills during the class and the hour class soon became a day spent together walking and talking. He was an avid photographer and soon she became the principal subject of his photographs, and that winter he invited her to concerts and the theater. They enjoyed each other's company as they were both culture lovers and had similar tastes. For him it was a new experience to discuss books, plays, and world views with a woman who could hold her own and was not too shy to disagree. But my father wasn't rushing into anything and was very aware of their age difference. So it took him until early 1939 to invite her to join him on a bus tour of the beautiful mountains in northeastern Hungary. The trip was all very proper but also very romantic, so in late summer he invited her again, this time on a bus tour of Yugoslavia. Easy companionship turned into deepening love. In September he proposed and she accepted. On September 28, 1939 they married in a simple ceremony, followed by a dinner presided over by his mother for the eight close family members present. After the dinner the couple left for a weekend honeymoon at a hotel in the Buda hills. When they arrived, she found the room filled with her favorite flowers.

The only person unhappy with the situation was my father's mother, Laura. She disapproved of his marrying at all, but especially of him marrying someone so much younger and not well off. She delivered her opinion to both of them, making my mother feel very unwelcome. Although my father was much influenced by his mother, she couldn't sway him. They married anyway. But Laura mama, as she wanted to be called, sat down her new daughter-in-law privately, extracting a promise from her that all of the Fleischl family jewelry would be inherited by his daughters, also insisting that he was most definitely too old to have his life disturbed by another child. I especially sat up and listened when Mother was telling me this. (Lucky for Laura mama, she died in 1942, before she knew of me or had to experience the Holocaust.)

Right after their marriage my parents were looking for a home, not wanting to live with his mother. Condominiums were a brand new concept in the late 1930s and my father was taken with the idea. They joined with five other families to finance the construction of a new building in the outskirts of Buda, in the lovely hilly district of Pasarét, where the air was good and there was a lot of greenery still. Since my father's kid brother and first wife died of tuberculosis, he was always worried that he and his daughters were especially susceptible. Good air was the only known prevention or cure at that time.

My parents had been married less than a year when my father was taken to a forced labor camp, but two months later those over fifty were released were released from that camp. They both saved the tender love letters they exchanged during those weeks of separation. Home from the labor camp in December 1940 my father found himself unemployed. The law that forbade Jews from holding professional jobs had been in effect for two years prior but had not been enforced because the economy could not afford to let go of that brain power. It wasn't until the end of 1940 that the pressure from Germany was so intense that all Jews were actually fired. My father went from respected chief financial officer to unemployed CPA scrambling to find private clients to support his wife and mother. But he was disciplined and confident and soon built a solid clientele. Life was good for a couple of years. The only cloud was the awareness of the growing hatred of Jews that felt like there was less and less air to breathe. But they could close their eyes and ears to the mounting anti-Jewish rhetoric and believe that what was happening in the neighboring countries would not come to Hungary. As she pasted into the anniversary album the tickets, photos, and the silly sweet poems of love and gratitude that they had written to each other, Mother recounted their bus trips to the country's beautiful spots to celebrate birthdays and anniversaries.

Then my mother found herself pregnant in the fall of 1943 with Hungary in a war that was going badly for their side and their situation as Jews ever more precarious. What to do? She already had two abortions at the insistence of Laura mama and she longed for a baby. Luckily for me, my father was an optimist and said, "By the time the baby will be born it will be all over and we will be fine." When Mother got to this part, she remarked wryly, "A fortune teller your father was not."

I loved hearing these stories, which made my parents somehow more real. I worried and begged to go see Father, but the hospital had strict visiting hours, especially for children, so I was only allowed to see him a few times. The patients were in huge wards with twelve beds on each side along the wall, and it was scary. People looked so bad, coughing and groaning. But some were friendly and motioned me to come nearer and talk to them. One old lady looked like Grandmami and I approached her and caressed her brow. She smiled and patted my arm.

During my last visit, about a week before he died, I wanted to crawl in bed with Father but my mother didn't let me. His face looked so sunken. But he held my hand and asked me what I was doing in first grade and about my teacher. He smiled and told me to be a good student. Even though I knew about death from losing Grandmami, it did not occur to me that my father was actually dying.

Perhaps he hadn't known it either. When my parents'

anniversary came on September 28, my mother took to the hospital the album she had made for him. But he told her, "No, sweetheart, I don't want to see it in this place. I want to savor it when I come home." The next morning he died.

Late morning on September 29, 1950, the school custodian came to my classroom and whispered with the teacher. Then he told me to come with him, that I needed to go home. Neither he nor the teacher said more, they just sent me on my way alone. From not knowing, suddenly I knew with an inexorable certainty. The walk down Orso Street that I usually liked so much seemed long and gray. I climbed up the stairs of our house to the third floor, dragging myself up, not wanting to get there, looking at the white spackle on the light blue walls of the stairwell, holding on to the banister, going one stair at a time.

I don't remember who told me what. But I can see myself sitting on the unmade bed, with the gray mattresses standing upright, and my mother's sister Trudi sitting next to me, saying "You know, from now on you are the one who will have to take care of your mother." It might have been just something to say to distract a small child. But I knew clearly and unquestioningly that it was the truth and felt crushed under the weight of it.

I never saw my father's body and was not allowed to go to the cemetery for the burial. I have always wished I could have seen him, said goodbye, had an actual physical moment of separation rather than this aching, never-healing chasm that has dogged me through the years.

From Liberation to Communism

As my parents and sisters struggled over the five years from the end of the war, facing the irrevocable loss of death, finding strength in hope, and rebuilding their lives, the country was going through a parallel trajectory.

In 1945, while Christians and Jews concentrated on finding food and some kind of shelter, the first order of business for the country was restoration on a larger scale. Hungary had to rebuild its infrastructure, restart factories for the production of steel and building materials, jumpstart commerce in general, as well as rebuild the government and political life. Getting the country on its feet was made ten times harder by enormous war reparations imposed on by the victors, to be paid to the Soviet Union, Czechoslovakia and Yugoslavia. The Allied Control Commission (US, Britain and the USSR) was formed to oversee compliance. Since it had been the Soviet army that liberated and then occupied Hungary, the USSR by its continued physical presence had the most clout. The US and England were far more interested in Western Europe, and while they occasionally raised pro-forma protests, they mostly left the Soviet Union in charge and able to meddle in the emerging political and economic life of Hungary. There was to be no Marshall plan for us.

One of the first things the government did was to revoke the anti-Jewish laws, which had prevented Jews from working in the professions, owning property, and so forth. At the same time it legitimized the Communist Party and exonerated the leftists who were persecuted between the two world wars. That these two government acts happened at the same time unfortunately served to reinforce the association in people's mind between Jews and communists and thus to feed an anti-Semitism that was not sated even by the Holocaust. The association of Jews and communism was not totally spurious. Many Jewish survivors saw in the communist ideals a hope for a humane society and a better world. Many joined the party, my mother's sister Trudi and several of our friends among them. In the yellow-star houses, where in 1944 the Jews were locked in for 22 out of every 24 hours, the old gathered to remember better times and to lament, but the young, like my cousin Ancsa and many like her, gathered to discuss how to survive and to envision a world that was not hostile to them, that was worth living in and working for. When it was all over those who survived came out eager to join the party and build a better world.

Although there were plenty of Hungarians who wanted to simply restore the Kingdom of Hungary and life as it had been, most of those involved in politics looked to the West and envisioned a parliamentary democracy establishing the "Republic of Hungary." A multitude of parties cropped up, but soon they were generally aligned into two camps. The "left" was led by the Communist Party and included the Social Democrats (to which a majority of the urban professionals and intellectuals belonged, as well as most of the Jews). The "right" was led by the Smallholders Party (they represented rural owners of small and medium-size farms) and also contained the Christian Democrats (a party of the new Christian middle-class, artisans, small-shop owners, and bureaucrats, officially supported by the clergy).

The Communist Party, banned between the wars, grew in less than a year of legal existence to 500,000 members. But they were by no means a majority. In a field with many parties, the Smallholders Party won absolute majority in the first elections. The net result of the first election was polarization. Although they didn't win, the parties on the left received 43 percent of the votes and gained a lot of clout, especially with the continuing presence of the Red Army and the ability of the Soviet Union to meddle in internal affairs.

The communists did not hide their intentions. At the 1946 party congress they declared their aim to create a socialist system in Hungary, following the political and economic model of the USSR. However, it appeared they were willing to bide their time within the established political system. As a first step, they managed to gain control of the executive branch and the security organizations, while the Smallholders held the majority in the Assembly, the legislative body. Holding executive power, the communists were able to get rid of the more conservative, middle-class members of the Smallholders party leadership (as well as the more moderate or nationalistic members of the

Communist Party) by accusing them of "conspiracy against the Republic" and mounting show trials. For example, the Prime Minister, who was of the majority Smallholders party, was indicted while on vacation abroad, discouraging him from coming home. It was a simple way to save the trouble of trying him and creating more animosity.

While the communists maneuvered, politics were not top on most people's minds—although maybe they should have been. The need for food, shelter and fuel felt so much more immediate. Inflation was spiraling absurdly out of control. People would receive their pay (always in cash) and run to the store before going home; a couple of hours' delay might have meant a doubling in the price of bread. Pretty soon they had to go home first to get the wheelbarrow, because they couldn't carry the amount of *pengös* needed to buy a kilogram of bread. Finally the old currency was recalled and a new currency, the *forint*, was introduced in August 1946.

The new currency was more manageable, but there was precious little it could buy. The Soviet army stationed in Hungary had to be fed and otherwise supported first, which was the government's responsibility. The land reform gave small parcels of land to farmers, but they had no means to acquire tractors and other machinery for efficient farming, so production was slow. Food rationing was introduced and with it a thriving black market blossomed. Those who dared ate better. You could always find food if you could go to the farmer or sausage maker directly. In the country you could have a few chickens, grow vegetables, feed a pig.

The scarcities people suffered, especially city people,

needed to be blamed on something or somebody. Once again, Jews became the target. From simple accusations that Jewish shop owners were dealing on the black market (who didn't if they could?), the rumors went back to primitive absurd tales of Jews picking up and killing Christian children. Jews outside of Budapest who had survived by some miracle the Holocaust now faced roving lynch mobs. Several were hung, others were beaten to death.

Added to the problem of scarcities was the establishment of war crime tribunals. The less-educated Christian country people, steeped in the virulent pre-war propaganda, had seen nothing wrong in collaborating with the Germans nor in ridding themselves of Jews, whom they believed to be the cause of their poverty and of the nation's troubles. They saw the war crime tribunals as a pretext for the surviving Jewish community to exact revenge. Incidents such as the smashing of the windows of the synagogue in the beautiful city of Pécs, where some of the tribunals were held, were not uncommon. In a perfect vicious circle, those experiences reinforced the Jews' belief that only a communist regime would want to protect them.

It wasn't until 1947, two years after the war ended, that representatives of Hungary and the Allies signed the final peace treaty in Paris. Hungary renounced all territories gained during World War II, going back to the frontiers set out by the hated 1920 Treaty of Trianon (by which Hungary lost two-thirds of its territory after WWI). People expected that after the signing of the peace treaty the Soviet Army would leave the country and the country would become truly independent. But that's not what happened. Instead, in frequent consultation with Moscow, the Hungarian communists got rid of the opposition through their two-pronged approach: instilling fear and suspicion, and working on gaining the hearts and minds of the people through propaganda. They moved inexorably toward a centralized economic system, starting with the nationalization of the coal mines and heavy industries already in 1946. The people didn't seem to worry too much about it; it made sense that the government could do a better job coordinating these complex but essential areas for the country's recovery. Besides, the shareholders of these large concerns were extremely rich and elicited little sympathy from the people struggling to feed and clothe themselves and keep warm.

During September 1947, the communists made a bold play to win the elections. Although they didn't dominate the legislature, earlier in the year they managed to pressure enough representatives to pass a law declaring those of German origin and those belonging to extreme-right parties before 1945 ineligible to vote, thus eliminating some of their opposition. Equally important, another law enabled people with absentee ballots to vote at any polling station. The communists orchestrated voting brigades and got about 60,000 illegal votes, through absentee ballots. But when the count was over they found that it wasn't enough. The moderate coalition received over 50 percent of the votes and the semblance of a pluralistic political system was left intact. People felt relieved and they went about the business of daily life. Only looking back was it clear that if they ever had a chance to prevent a takeover, it was probably already too late by then, although it took another two years for the communists to succeed completely.

Following the elections which they lost, the communists took off the gloves. They organized a merger of all left-leaning parties into one big party, named the Hungarian Workers Party (perhaps less off-putting than "communist party") and in a cunning strategy the party leadership succeeded in reviving the Hungarian National Independence Front, the old alliance of parties and unions that formed the provisional government of 1945. They succeeded in convening a congress of the National Independence Front, and by fiat the congress changed the voting system so that those who stood for office in subsequent elections were no longer candidates of individual parties but of the Front. Thus people could only approve or vote down an entire slate, giving them no real choices. How did the people stand for it? It is hard to imagine. But the battle for people's hearts and minds was on, the rhetoric strident, the propaganda crude but powerful. By its own declaration, the Hungarian Workers Party was working tirelessly to look out for the interests of the workers and to get rid of perceived enemies everywhere. The world was viewed in the most simplistic terms: you were either an anti-imperialist democrat or an anti-democratic imperialist.

While democracy was loudly proclaimed, in fact democracy was over. In the May 1949 elections the National Front (read communist) candidates received—to nobody's surprise—96 percent of the votes.

The Hungarian Workers Party became the only party and in August 1949 the Republic of Hungary became the

People's Republic of Hungary, "a state of the proletariat and working peasants" where "all power belongs to the people." A new constitution was signed on August 20, which was St. Stephen's day, the commemoration of the coronation of the first king of Hungary and a traditional national holiday. It was a clever move; the popular holiday could continue to be observed but celebrating the constitution without mention of kings or saints.

Mátyás Rákosi, an old communist from the brief 1919 regime, who spent twenty-five years in the Soviet Union, returned to Hungary in 1945 and was appointed Secretary General of the Communist Party, and in 1949 of the new Hungarian Workers Party, the most powerful position as the party gained total power. He proudly claimed to be "Stalin's best pupil"—and he proved it in the following four years.

The nationalization of banks, industries, and media occurred fast. By December 1949 there was no private sector. The peasants who had just obtained their farms through the 1945 land reform had little joy from it. By 1949-50 they were coerced to enter collectives. The grocery stores (all bearing the same name in the entire country and only distinguished by a number) were stocked by the government and prices were centrally determined.

The communists realized that they needed to win the intellectual adherence of a critical mass of people and that the way to do that was through education, the media, and the arts. They set about it both with a naïve faith and with a ruthless efficiency that often backfired. First they targeted the schools. Already in June of 1948 they nationalized all church-run schools. The nuns and monks who had done most of the elementary and secondary teaching up to then were offered posts in the now public schools, but Cardinal Mindszenty forbade them from accepting the offer. That created an enormous teacher shortage. Despite the shortage, the government changed the four-grade elementary schools system to eight grades and declared elementary school education compulsory, with high school or vocational school free but not mandatory.

University also was free, and those wanting to become teachers were given stipends and all kinds of incentives. But these education aspirations came up against the reality that many university professors had died in the war or concentration camps, others had left the country while they could, and still others were not allowed to teach because of their "untrustworthy class background." Soon it had become clear that the numbers of high school and university students had to be limited because there were neither sufficient schools nor enough teachers to provide this ambitious free education to everyone immediately. Advantage was given to those who came from worker or peasant families. It became another *numerus clausus* (cap on numbers) for the Jews—first they couldn't attend the university because they were Jews, and now they couldn't attend because they usually came from merchant or more educated backgrounds. But I could not understand people's anger about this. I found it hard to reject the argument that if the pie is limited, those who have been hungry the longest should eat first. When it came to education, those were the children of workers and peasants.

While waging an all-out campaign to win people's devotion, such as with free education, the government also copied Soviet paranoia and terror. Rákosi, who kept personal authority over the AVO (secret police) launched a campaign with the slogan "Increase Vigilance!" inciting people to look everywhere for enemies of the state, enemies of the workers, to "watch out for the smallest hostile actions or words." People were encouraged to report on their fellow workers, friends, and family. All dissent, even potential, was mercilessly dealt with. The Soviet approach of spectacular party purges was adopted. Show trials run by the government or the party—there was no clear way to separate them—on trumped up charges against leaders of the Hungarian Workers Party who didn't quite toe the line ended up with imprisonment or execution of faithful, idealist communists. This was also an expedient way for Rákosi to get rid of perceived rivals. The most famous of these purges was against former interior minister László Rajk, who was executed, and János Kádár, who first followed Rajk as interior minister but a year later was also tried and imprisoned. Alive or dead, they came to play an important role later on.

The western border was firmly closed with miles of barbed wire and thousands of machine-gun toting Russian and Hungarian soldiers. The iron curtain came down. And so we went in less than five years from liberation: from the Allies (in our case the Soviets) literally saving our lives, to the battle to reconstruct the country, and finally to another era of fear and scarcity, ensnared by another bondage.

Life Without Father

We felt the pervasive fear and dearth of daily necessities as much as others. But foremost we lived in our own drama, punctuated by the relief of ordinary life. After Father's death, Mother was devastated and hysterical with fear. Fear, because the deportations continued and the general atmosphere was one of dread, but even more so because we were so alone. She was a forty-three year old widow with a six-year-old child, faced with the necessity of building a new life and finding a way to support us.

Eva and Márta grieved with us. But they had their own lives, and their own grave difficulties, especially Eva, with her seven-year-old Gábor. We did not see them often, at least not as often as I would have liked. We saw more of my mother's sister Trudi but she, too, was on the periphery. She was someone whom my mother asked for advice, someone to buck her up and try to instill some common sense in her, but not part of our daily life. We were essentially on our own.

Mother grieved for Father fiercely and with a naked pain. She cried, railed, stormed. She kept asking, "What will we do?" I had no answers. Despite my aunt Trudi's charge that now I had to take care of my mother, her fear and seeming helplessness terrified me. If she didn't know what we were going to do, what could I do? What would happen to us? It was all so unreal. I felt numb. I still saw Father in the hospital, his gentle wave of the hand as we left.

We were in our room on the morning of October 29, the one-month anniversary of my father's death, when the bell rang. Mother went to open the door but found nobody on the other side. The ringing continued. At last we noticed that the dining room chair had been pushed against the little bell that rang in the kitchen, but there was nobody else there who could have pushed the chair. It defied logic. Mother became convinced that Father's spirit had came to comfort and encourage us, and I liked that idea very much. We felt strengthened. She slowly started looking seriously at our options.

Since she had given private English lessons before, tutoring was a natural place to start. She found a couple of students who wanted to learn English. The official attitude toward English was one of the system's many contradictions. Although listening to western radio was forbidden, and in general learning English was looked upon with suspicion (and was therefore risky), the government recognized that professionals, especially scientists and engineers and students in those fields, needed to know English in order to read the most recent, most advanced literature. One of the hospitals hired my mother to teach English to doctors from 7:00 to 9:00 every morning, before their regular day started. The word-of-mouth telegraph was always humming in Budapest, usually with political rumors, but it also served in this case. Soon Mother was giving private lessons to a few engineering students, followed by two high school seniors hoping to become physicists. It was a start.

Then one of her friends suggested she apply for a job to the National Translation and Interpretation Bureau. Like everything else by then, this type of work too was centralized, government run and controlled. Since my mother spoke English, German, and French besides Hungarian, and since there were not many people left alive and not deported who had these skills, she got hired immediately. She was buoyed and encouraged but also scared. She had never worked with other people and she had never worked in an office before.

She was not comfortable translating into French or Hungarian, because she felt less sure of the thoroughness of her knowledge of those languages, but translating into English or German from any of her other languages went well and she found that she enjoyed the work and the camaraderie of the office. After a while they started to give her interpreter assignments when foreign visitors came. That was much tenser work. She came home from those jobs exhausted, anxious, and short-tempered. Sometime in 1951, the head of an English labor union visited Hungary and Mother was assigned to escort him for several days, going to steel mills and factories, translating speeches about high productivity and about how wonderful the life of the workers was in Hungary. She kept toying with the idea of telling in English what was really going on, rather than the glowing things the Hungarians were telling her to say. But she never did because she was terrified that they might be testing her, that a Hungarian would understand her or that the English visitor, probably a communist, would report her and she would go to prison. She came home a nervous wreck every night that week.

She also started to rant and rave, often to the point of losing control, reminiscing about the Holocaust, going over the harrowing experiences, reliving them in every detail. The anxiety and pressure she was under somehow opened that dam, or maybe earlier she would relive those days with my father. But now she mostly had only me to talk to about it, and after a while I felt like I had experienced it all too. Of course, I did as a baby, and might not babies remember in a curious way, in their flesh? The baby experience now became fused with my mother's endless reliving and in horrible nightmares.

There were sweeter reminiscences about my father, as well. She was concerned that I would forget him, and she had her own need to conjure him so she talked a lot about him. I loved the stories and built an image of my perfect father. Nevertheless I was glad when a few years later my sisters told me more about him, so I could have some sense of the real man.

First grade passed in a blur. I wasn't engaged with it or with the other children. I liked my solitary walk to school along the six blocks on Orso Street, its narrow sidewalk put together with scored stone slabs that looked like big tiles. I made a game of getting to school never stepping on a line between the squares. The school was a big ochre-colored building with a green iron fence, looking rather like the nearby military barracks. A couple who lived in an apartment attached to school took care of the building and kept an eye on our comings and goings. The school had only four grades and maybe a hundred and twenty students, so they knew us all. The wide paved area in front of the building was used for assemblies and recess play, and for the perennial soccer, which I dreaded. I didn't like the ball hurtling towards me and couldn't keep from lifting my arms to shield my head. I clearly wasn't soccer material.

Shortly after my father's death, the government issued a regulation designed to solve the severe housing shortage in Budapest. It allowed families only one room, not one apartment. We had two bedrooms, a windowless dining room, and a tiny room off the kitchen. To avoid being forced to share the apartment with total strangers, my mother invited a friend of a friend, 60-year-old Mária Bérczi, who needed a place to live, to sublet my father's old room. Before the war Mr. and Mrs. Bérczi owned a lace store in the fashionable Váci Street, but the store was lost in the war. Her husband had been killed by the Nazis, her adult son and daughter lived in England. She was a dignified and cultured woman, with a sense of humor that she hadn't lost even after her harrowing experiences in the Holocaust. She and my mother immediately liked each other.

We still had the tiny room off the kitchen that was built to be a maid's room, though it had never been used as such. Mother found Claire for it right in our building. Mrs. Rónai and her daughter Claire, who lived in the ground-floor apartment, were the wonderful people who saved our things and looked out for our apartment during the Holocaust. Now Mrs. Rónai wanted her married daughter,

Gizi, with her husband and their four children to come live in their place. So spinster daughter Claire came to live upstairs giving us a truly full house even in the eyes of the District Council.

Maria Bérczi, it turned out, was awaiting trial because she had tried to cross the border illegally to join her children, and trying to leave after 1949 was considered treason. She was caught, actually betrayed by the person to whom she had paid all of her money to smuggle her across the Hungarian-Austrian border. After living with us for a few months she was finally sentenced to one year in prison. Because she wanted to join her children and be with her grandchildren, whom she had never met, this diminutive arthritic lady was sent to a work-prison, where she had to collect mulberry leaves and feed silk worms in a rough, cold, damp building way out in the countryside.

With her leaving we had an empty room and were again in danger of having the District Council put a stranger in that room. Fortunately, old Mrs. Rónai was happy to have a quiet room of her own away from her grandchildren and moved up. Since Gizi and Miklós had four children and a fifth on the way, they were entitled to the whole two-room apartment. Besides, he was a mining engineer, an expertise highly prized, so he was entitled to more privileges as well as extra pay for a "dangerous occupation." We were much luckier than many people we knew, who had a lot of trouble and conflict with the people whom they asked into, or who were put into, their apartments under the new rule. It was easy to have Mrs. Rónai living with us because she spent most of the day in the apartment with Gizi and her grandchildren and didn't use our kitchen. So although we never went into her room the apartment didn't feel that crowded. Also her daughter Claire was quiet as a mouse, just a shadow tiptoeing around. I heard my mother comment that Claire really wanted to be a nun, but that wasn't possible in these times. She spent much of her time in the church across the street from us.

When Mária Bérczi was released from prison in the spring of 1952, she was very ill with pneumonia and had nowhere to go. I was afraid she would die like Grandmami. So Mother offered her the small dining room to sleep in (we weren't obliged to have anyone live there because it didn't have a window) and she essentially lived with us. She became a good friend and support to my mother. Her laughter at the absurdities that were going on around us were a kind of balance to my mother, who always saw herself as a tragic heroine. Mother gave her the nickname "Móri" and that's what we called her. She was tiny, and had a round face, round glasses, and a lovely smile. She not only had a wonderful wry sense of humor but was warm and loving. I liked her a lot, yet at the same time often resented her. She was a stranger, not my family, yet always there. I oscillated between rage and desolation that I didn't dare to express but felt eating away my insides. I wanted my father. I wanted a mother who was there. I wanted a life like I imagined the other families in the building had. But I knew that if I said anything to my mother, she would be the one enraged, telling me what an ungrateful child I was. So one day when Móri told me to wash the dishes I exploded at her, saying "You are not my mother and you better never tell me what to do." But Móri was patient and calm and slowly she became a beloved, steady presence, a second grandmother to me.

The one room we lived in became very crowded, with Father's big desk that we brought in from the room occupied by Mrs. Rónai dominating it. Mother and I shared the double bed, sleeping crosswise, to leave more room between us. I don't know how her feet didn't dangle down, but I was small enough that it felt cozy. As I was falling asleep, I loved to touch the satiny smooth foot board and look at the pattern of the wood, light brown woven through with darker threads. There were two large armoires matching the bed and where they met in the corner stood a smooth black, lazy-susan-like linen closet. It was my parents' marriage furniture that had survived the war when strangers lived in our apartment.

At the foot-end of the bed there was an upright piano, leaving barely enough room to pass to the bathroom, which in typical European fashion did not have the toilet in it. The toilet was a tiny, always freezing closet at the other side of the entrance hall. Toilet paper rarely was obtainable, so I (and many others) spent time cutting up our newspaper to use. Kneeling on the bookshelf under the big window of our room, I could see far to houses and tree tops, and daydream about my father, about the siblings I would like to have, and very often about food.

Food occupied my mind in direct measure to what wasn't in my stomach. I was hungry pretty much all the time. At school, after classes we were served lunch and then had play time and homeroom to do our homework.

Lunch came in big aluminum vats and was some kind of thick soup, usually pea, bean or lentil. For a lot of us it was the only real meal, and I prayed that enough kids would be out sick so I could get a second plateful. My mother also received a noon-time meal at work.

Often I was the one who was sick. I missed half of second grade because I got one childhood illness after the other: whooping cough, measles and I don't remember what else, as well as several bad ear infections. The city was divided into districts, and there were district doctor's offices. Our district doctor lived and worked just on the other side of the Pasaréti Square and was a family friend, which made it easier. All medical treatment was free, but just as there weren't enough teachers, there was a scarcity of medical facilities. The district doctors many times, as in our case, were old house doctors who knew and cared about their patients.

Having to stay home alone when sick, I amused myself by creating pages of patterns on my mother's old manual typewriter combining the little symbols above the numbers. I also had a set of beautiful, flat wooden blocks of different shapes, lacquered in red, yellow, blue, and green, that my mother's oldest sister, Mila had sent from the US in 1948 when that was still possible. Those blocks were my treasure and I happily consumed hours creating shapes and color combinations. I also discovered the fun of reading while trying to cure my earache sitting more or less still with my ear close to a lit bulb and let the heat radiate in (a common remedy at that time).

In the summer the ear infections disappeared and I

relished being outside, playing in the garden, around the beds of flox and snapdragons. The garden sloped down toward Pasaréti Square, where the food store, toiletries store, pharmacy, tabak, and a few other stores were, as well as the terminal of the number five bus, all coming together in what seemed to me a stone wreath around the circle of flowers that surrounded the statue of the Virgin Mary. The house, the garden, the square were my little domain. Sometimes I wandered our hilly neighborhood, rolling down the grassy field at the end of our street and making dandelion garlands, finding apples, and climbing a neighbor's cherry tree. The flowers and trees were the colors in our life, amidst the drabness.

There were no means to repair or repaint the buildings pockmarked by bullet holes and scarred by chunks of missing plaster, clothes were mostly utilitarian and dark colored, and the few cars that we saw were all black. Nature burst in to uplift our monochromatic world and I loved the flowering fruit trees, the delicious smell of the lilac bushes, the forsythia, and the bridal wreath with its tiny white clusters, the grass, the early lilies of the valley and violets, the cosmos and the peonies. I delighted in them all.

Sometimes on Sundays, the only day my mother didn't work, we would take the tram and go to János mountain (really more of a hill) and walk to the lookout tower to see beautiful Budapest. From the distance it wasn't the ruined buildings that stood out but the hilly terrain, the silver thread of the Danube spanned by graceful bridges, and the view of the exquisite gothic Parliament on the Pest shore. On those excursions Mother would often tell wistful stories

The buildings not made unhabitable by bombing and not on main streets did not get repaired for decades. Walking by such building was a common yet disquieting experience.

about her parents and sisters and their younger years. I eagerly put together these stories, the ones my mother told me when she was making the anniversary album for my father, the stories of her childhood, of her as a young woman. Occasionally Trudi would tell me family stories too and with each story I put together a more complete picture of my family. Even knowing that there was once a large family, a different life, felt good.

There was indeed once a large and happy family. Mother's father, Julius Donner, was one of eight children and had come from a fairly well-to-do family that sent him to Vienna to study in the 1890s. There he found a job in a bank where he worked his way up. He also found in Vienna his love, my grandmother, Bertha Schulz, the daughter of a family of modest means. Bertha was one of six children, and when they met she was working in a millinery shop.

Shortly after their wedding, the bank sent my grandfather to Bucharest, Rumania, to establish a branch of the bank. They lived there in style, he being the director of the bank branch, and had their first two children, Mila and Gertrude (Trudi). My grandfather was so successful that after a few years the bank in Vienna decided to send him on to establish another branch in Sofia, Bulgaria. There my mother, Marianne, was born in 1907. Mila and Trudi, seven and five, adored and indulged this new arrival, and of course lorded it over her. They dressed her up as a doll, they played games with her, she sat in their classes with the governess, they taught her to climb trees. As the bank became well established in Sofia, Julius felt his work there was done and was considering moving back to Vienna. But then a bank in Budapest made him an offer so good he couldn't refuse and the family moved to Budapest in 1914.

All through those moves it was as if the family had never left Vienna. They spoke German, and the girls had German and French governesses as was the custom for cultured and well off families. My mother spoke of her childhood as idyllic. Their social life revolved mostly around the extended family. They spent time in Vienna every year, visiting grandparents, uncles and aunts, and cousins. Family members visited back and forth constantly. Between Julius' parents, seven siblings and their families, and Bertha's mother, five siblings and their families, they were sufficient onto themselves. The three girls adored their mother's sisters and brother. They also spent fun summers with their father's sister Linka and her husband, who had a big cheese-making operation in the small Hungarian city of Tamási. Aunt Linka and Uncle Andrew were kind people and not at all strict. The girls could play unsupervised and make friends with the kids of the neighborhood, something not allowed at home. Years later Mother and I reconnected with one of those playmates from the Tamási summers, and he became important in our lives.

The year the family moved to Budapest World War I broke out. The war had not affected my mother's family directly, but by the time it was over in 1919 the circumstances had changed in Vienna so that her father saw no particular reason to return. They bought and remodeled a beautiful mansion in Buda and ended up spending the rest of their lives in Hungary, although neither my grandmother, nor my mother or her sister Mila ever felt at home there. Only her sister Trudi embraced the country wholeheartedly. She insisted on going to a Hungarian school, spoke the language beautifully, and loved to read the works of Hungarian writers and poets.

My grandfather's star rose with the bank's and he became involved in the establishment of several commercial and manufacturing ventures. He built a considerable fortune, being a shrewd investor and a popular manager. During the brief communist regime in 1919, the government wanted to take him hostage along with other high ranking industrialist and financial leaders. But he was so popular with the workers of the company he was presiding over that they barred the government officials and insisted that he be allowed to continue to lead the company.

The Donner family was not religious. When Julius perceived that there would be an anti-Jewish backlash after the end of the war in 1919, he had the whole family convert to Catholicism. They all had to go to several Catechism classes, but rationalists as they were, they just went along with what was deemed necessary. Except for my mother. Her imagination and spirit caught fire, and she became a devoted Catholic. The family was amused by this and she got teased a great deal, which she hated. More than anything, she wanted to be taken seriously.

Mother didn't feel socially adept or athletic as a young girl. She was told that she was pretty, though the beauty of the family was

My mother in her early twenties.

her oldest sister, Mila. She liked to play the piano, and read French, German, and English romantic works, fantasizing about being the adored heroine or about sacrificing herself for a noble cause. Eventually her parents sent her to Oxford to study. Oxford's dreamy spires matched her disposition, and the English temperament suited her well. She met many new people from all over the world. Since she was educated by private tutors and had never gone to school or studied with peers, she had never had the satisfaction of discussing ideas in this kind of larger, expansive venue. It was new, exciting, and liberating. She got invited to some English country homes and adored that lifestyle. Mother's eyes would sparkle as she told me about the years in Oxford, how they were some of the best of her life.

But when she had her diploma in hand, twenty-four year old Marianne had to return home to bad news. During the economic depression that had set in in Budapest her father had lost most of his fortune in stocks and various investments. To top it off, fascinated by technical innovation, he had invested heavily in several new inventions that did not pan out. He tried to recover unsuccessfully for a couple of years, but by 1935 it was clear that they were totally broke and owed a lot of money.

Creditors came and went. Beautiful things were sold. The mansion became barer and barer. But perhaps due to his standing in the community and the good that he had done, his creditors were also kind to seriously ill Julius. The family was allowed to remain in their home until he died in July of 1937. Then my mother and grandmother moved to an apartment on the opposite side of the street, within view of their old mansion. (Why so close, I wondered listening to my mother. Even my eight-year-old brain knew that I wouldn't want to do that.) The newspapers printed glowing tributes to my grandfather that did not mention his downfall, but spoke of the commercial and industrial concerns he established, the important role he had in financial institutions all over Eastern Europe, of his "stupendous" work as the director of the Budapest Bank. They spoke of him as the "angel" of inventors, and praised his humility and support of others. It was a salve for the sore souls of his wife and daughter, who, with losing him, lost their home too. (The two older daughters were already married and out on their own.)

This was the first time that the practical survivor had to rise in Mother (and a good thing that she didn't know in how many difficult times she would have to rise again). She hated what she considered her humiliation of losing their wealth and standing, and never got over the loss of the life she had once had, but in the moment of need she was able to push all that aside and act. She put the word out that she was looking for private students who wanted to learn English. And so she met my father who came to refresh his knowledge of English.

My mother told some of these family stories over and over, and I listened hungrily for new details. I dreamed about playing with cousins in Tamási, about having all those aunts and uncles, and tried to imagine what it would be like to grow up with seven sisters and brothers like grandfather had. Those outings where Mother would talk about her past and not the Holocaust were the good times. She would be dreamy and teary but calm, and I really treasured calm. Life at home was a scary roller coaster. Mother was always exhausted after the long hours she worked and her emotional state was precarious. Her volatile temper got the better of her often, especially with me. She lost control at the slightest provocation and a spell of fury would overtake her; then she would scream, slap me or if I wasn't at arms reach, throw the dictionary or whatever book was handy at my head. Sometimes when that happened I would go wordlessly and bring her a tranquilizer and some water. It was my way of coping and perhaps shaming her out of her fury.

What made me really mad was when I felt she was unjust. Like the day a friend of hers was coming up the stairs and a stone fell down the stairwell, almost hitting the woman. Mother was convinced that I had thrown the stone down on purpose, even though I assured her that I hadn't touched it. But when she got into a state you couldn't argue with her. She knew that I didn't like the lady, so she had put two and two together and came up with five. She grabbed me by the neck and kept banging my head against the wall until her friend yelled, "Marianne, stop, you'll kill her!" and she came to her senses.

Another time in second grade a schoolmate invited me to her house. I was hardly ever invited to any of my classmates so I was thrilled. As luck would have it a really bad storm broke out and the girl's mother wouldn't allow me to go home, no matter how much I begged her. I knew there would be trouble if my mother came home and didn't find me there but I didn't know what to do. My poor mother had to go out in the drenching rain in the middle of the night to get me. No matter how many times I told her I couldn't help it, she did not speak to me for days. Her cold fury I dreaded more than the hot one. But most of all I hated with my whole being the unfairness of it all.

Yet even so I knew that she loved me, that I was her reason for keeping going. I understood she was terrified—terrified that we would be deported or she would be imprisoned, terrified of losing me, terrified of not being able to feed us. I sensed her terror and her tenuous hold on herself. If I didn't understand it then, looking back it is clear that for us to have survived she did a heroic job, even if my life with her was anything but easy.

Móri was a warm, even presence for me. Most often the only person there when I came home, she sat and knitted with her hands crippled with arthritis and was always ready to smile at me. The nights when my mother went to a student's home to teach English she would come very late and it was good to have Móri in the other room as I went to bed alone. Although Mother had her job in the translation bureau, she continued teaching at the hospital and had several private students. Sometimes students came to our home, staying until 10:00 pm. Since we had but the one room, she had to teach them where I played and slept. Later I would be grateful for the familiarity of the sounds of English.

Aunt Fodi and I in 1957.

Besides Móri my other mainstay was "Aunt Fodi." Fodi was a nickname that I gave to Mrs. Fodor, who came three times a week for a few hours to help out after Aunt Juszti got too old and tired and couldn't come anymore. Although everybody was poor, there were still peasant women in Budapest who earned their living as domestic help and there were still people who would forego other necessities and found the money to pay them. People utterly depended on them. I think it was a complicated symbiotic relationship. The one received nurturance and much needed help, and the other received respect, gratitude, and validation, in addition to a small income. Considering that we were in debt up to our ears I don't know how we paid her, but Fodi was a kind, strong old woman whom I loved and who loved me. She had the most wrinkled face I ever saw, smiling brown eyes, and always wore a kerchief on her head in the manner of old Hungarian peasant women and shoes that laced up midway her calves. When she was around I stayed out in the kitchen with her as much as possible, often the coziest and warmest spot in the house. She let me help her make soup or put the laundry on the lines of the drying frame that you could lower from the ceiling of the kitchen and then pull up again. The ceiling was tall and the laundry could hang without interfering with cooking or eating.

Our apartment had a kind of central heating: a large coal stove inside the wall where Father's room, our room, and the dining room met. It was covered on each side by nice creamy yellow tiles and was supposed to provide radiant heat. But because coal was very expensive and scarce we had to put a small stove in our room that required much less. The coal was stored in the basement, three flights down, in separate bins for each apartment. It became my job to bring up the coal in a bucket and clean the stove when I came home.

The basement, a short flight of stairs down from the main entrance, was dark and scary. Besides the storage and coal bins it contained a large, dank room that was the shared laundry room for all seven apartments, with big stone vats for washing and rinsing the heavy laundry. A window at ground level at the back of the building was the only ventilation. It could be closed from the yard by a rusted-out old iron cover with thick hinges and a heavy lever. My mother's reliving of the Holocaust took hold of my imagination and in many of my nightmares, for years to come, the Nazis inhabited the laundry room and I had to struggle to try to close the cover, or else I was hiding in the scary dark room and the Nazis locked the window cover to trap me in. The laundry room was also where Dr. Mengele would lure me to cut me up to see how Jews were made different.

But the basement also led to a good place: the Réfi family's door. I loved our concierge family. Not just my playmate, Anti, and his beautiful little sister, Marika, but his parents, big bosomed and round-faced Aunt Réfi and skinny Uncle Réfi in his worn work clothes and stubble of a beard always but on Sundays. Occasionally they invited me into the apartment to play. Sometimes I would sit in Uncle Réfi's lap pretending that he was my father. But that felt not quite right and a little disloyal. Mostly I sat outside on their tin-covered window-sill, which was accessible from the garden and was cold in the winter and hot in the summer. From there I could look into the kitchen and chatter with Aunt Réfi while she was cooking. Mrs. Réfi was kind, and if I was there at mealtime she gave me some too. Uncle Réfi sometimes drank and spanked the kids but knew a lot

With Aunt and Uncle Réfi, my friend Anti, and his sister Marika, at their kitchen window in 1957.

of mysterious things like building toy cars and raising rabbits and chickens in cages in the back of the garden. So they had meat when those of us who had to buy it didn't. While I couldn't watch when Uncle Réfi killed a rabbit or chicken, I observed carefully how Aunt Réfi cleaned it, using every bit of it. She even collected the blood and then cooked it to a solid consistency. We loved its sausage-like taste and smooth consistency. It never occurred to us that it was nasty.

My mother was somewhat amused at my "proletarian" friendship, because although she always preached "noblesse oblige," that our education, enlightenment, and advantages obliged us to respect others regardless of class, and that true talent and honesty was what was important, she couldn't quite shake her background. Little did she understand how I would have loved to truly belong to that blessedly normal family. But Hungary was, despite all communist preaching of the time, or maybe because of it, still very class conscious. It wasn't only my mother who viewed my attachment to the Réfis with amusement, but they did too. I think they also had a feeling that my friendship "graced" them, and therefore their acceptance of me was perhaps tinged with a certain resentment, which I picked up on. The hunger to belong could not really be satisfied.

Neither could physical hunger, except on a rare occasion. No matter how poor they were, country people could at least raise their own food. In second grade my school class had an outing to a little village not far from Budapest. I don't remember anything about the outing except that some generous peasant women gave us fried chicken, which

I can still smell and taste, the most heavenly fried chicken ever.

Then, sometime close to Christmas 1952, Aunt Fodi took me down to see her folks in the country, where they were doing a "pig killing." After an exciting train ride we were picked up in a hay wagon. I don't think I was ever as cold before or after than during that hay ride. It was a bitter cold and humid winter and I didn't have a warm coat. When we finally got to their place in the next village, to my great relief the pig was already slaughtered. All the activity was outdoors—music, lots of fires, and lots of people. In a cauldron the fat was being rendered, and in it big, glorious pieces of meat were frying. No pork has ever tasted so good to me. Then I was put down in a cold, cold room under a wonderful huge eiderdown. Next day we went back, and— oh glory!—we took some meat and sausages home with us.

Having Móri live with us provided another source of food and some clothing: the IKKA. I don't know what the letters stood for, but it was the means for relatives abroad to send us things. Nothing could be sent directly, but the country needed foreign currency so they allowed relatives to send dollars, which the government kept and in exchange allowed the recipient to pick from a list of food items or clothing and other goods. One had to wonder how come these were available for dollars but not in the regular stores, but at that time all we cared about was that it gave us cocoa, coffee, butter, and other such wonders. Móri's son and daughter, who lived in England, sent her money monthly. She never saw the money but got a notification that she could spend so much from the IKKA catalogue. She shared what she got with us as a sort of rent payment. She would also get skeins of wool and then knit sweaters for sale, laboriously but cheerfully with her gnarled misshapen fingers.

When not in school, the neighborhood kids made a sport of watching the government grocery and toiletries stores at Pasaréti Square. If we spotted a truck arriving at either, we would run home and to the neighbors we liked, ring their bells and let them know there was something at the store. Everyone who was at home hurried to line up in a queue. Nobody cared what was being delivered, because since everything was scarce, we knew we wanted it. It was like a mystery sweepstake: often it was mere potatoes, but sometimes we really lucked out and were able to buy butter, eggs, or toilet paper. Mother was never there, but I had household money and stood in line too, and she was pleased when she got home.

Whether running around with the neighborhood kids, most of them a couple of years older, or at school, I never quite belonged. I knew it and the others sensed it, even though we couldn't put it into words. It felt to me as if all the other kids belonged to a very desirable club of which I was left out. I was different. I didn't quite get why, but my feeling of not belonging was deepened by leading a double or triple life: ostensibly Catholic, secretly Jewish, officially nonreligious. Catholicism was my religion but I knew I was also Jewish. I had a vague understanding that Judaism was a religion too, but it was something else for us. It was simply who we were, something we didn't choose. An identity. A mysterious body knowledge that made us comfortable with some people and not others. Something that many people around us didn't like. It was something that nobody could find out about, a dangerous secret. Mother was very clear on that. Then there were those who couldn't find out about the Catholic part because a good communist couldn't be religious. Yet most people around us were quite religious, and if you were not they didn't trust you either. It was all enormously confusing.

The Catholic part was full of intrigue. Mother wouldn't dare to go to the church that was opposite to our house because she was afraid of losing her job. People with "good" (that is, working-class) backgrounds could allow themselves to defy the communist ideology better, but those of us of "questionable" (educated) backgrounds had to really watch our step. Mother was a devout Catholic and she would take me on the tram on some Sundays to a far-away church where nobody would know us. But I was allowed to go to the church across the street sometimes by myself, as she reasoned that nobody could expect her to control me. I resonated with the mysterious solemnity of Mass and felt peaceful with the old women reciting the rosary. The pomp and gravity of the neighborhood Easter procession moved me especially.

Not all was gravity. We also celebrated Easter by dying three or four eggs (any egg was a treat) and—having hit the jackpot earlier at the grocery store and procured a little butter—making cookies. On the Monday after Easter, according to the ancient Hungarian custom, the boys would come and sprinkle the girls with cologne, to which the girls had to respond by offering some goodies. It was an old courting custom in the countryside, but it spread to become a popular children's activity in the city. The boys of our building came and sprinkled me ceremonially, and I handed them a couple of cookies or a painted egg in return.

In the summer of 1952, when I was eight, Mother found a way to send me to Aunt Klara, a retired teacher who had a cottage along Lake Balaton where she summered kids. Again, how she paid for it I can't imagine, or rather, I know too well: she borrowed more money. It was the best two or three weeks I had ever had. The cottage was old and roomy with a porch and an overgrown garden. There were eight kids to play with and we walked to the lake every day.

The path to the beach traveled through wheat fields dotted with poppies. When there was a light breeze, the yellow wheat and the red poppies gently swayed in a dance of their own. The wheat was just ripening and we ran to pick a shaft, drink in its earthy smell and eat the tender wheat berries. I felt at home in the water and was not at all afraid even though I couldn't swim. When I was around five, my father had tried to teach me, and later so did Aunt Trudi, who was a great swimmer and beautiful diver, but I couldn't quite get it. It didn't matter much because the shore of the lake on the south side was shallow, and I could go in for quite a while before it became deep. The water was warm and the bottom of the lake was very smooth fine sand that spread between my toes, caressing my feet. Being in the lake was heavenly.

We also walked often to the train station by way of a little path bordered by the train tracks on one side and a forested hillside on the other. The sunlight through those trees created beautiful patterns illuminating the groundcover and the path. To me it was a magic, mysterious place. When my mother came down one weekend to visit, I watched for the train from the front of the cottage, and when I heard its whistle I ran like mad toward the train station. When she left, I watched for the train by the cottage looking for her and spotted her waving from the window.

I was able to go the next summer and then two years later. It was equally wonderful. For all my later life my stays in Balatonszemes, especially the walk to the lake and to the train station, came back in my dreams, filling me both with happiness and longing. But before my second summer at Lake Balaton, our and everyone else's life became a little lighter, a little more hopeful, when Stalin died on March 5, 1953.

The Worst Years of Communism

The three and a half years before Stalin died were the worst years of communism for us. I lived with hunger and absorbed the palpable fear around me. Although confused by all that I wasn't allowed to say outside our apartment, grown-ups often think kids can't hear so I picked up a lot from conversations around me. Only much later, determined to make sense of my memories, could I form a larger picture.

The main purveyor of fear, the spying agency known as AVO, operated as an autonomous organization, answering directly to Rákosi, the head of the Hungarian Workers Party. Although there was an outwardly functioning government with a national assembly, an executive, and a judiciary, in reality all power was concentrated in the party leadership, which dictated as well as oversaw the work of the government and all its agencies. The power of the party was omnipresent; its local neighborhood councils knew everyone and often received malicious information provided by neighbors with petty vendettas. The consequences for the people ratted on or falsely accused were dire; at best they would lose their jobs, but more often they were interned, or just disappeared. At the national level the party created an enemies list of old reactionaries and potential opponents. Rumor had it, and it was later confirmed, that over a million people—ten percent of the population—were on the list. A blanket of oppressive fear lay heavily on all of us.

Political show trials continued to be the way to get rid of critics of any idea or policy First Party Secretary Rákosi proposed, or was instructed to carry out by Moscow, where he often visited. Waves of purges followed each other; one morning a new person was named head of a department or ministry and extravagantly praised, a week or month later the paper carried a story of his being a traitor who would be tried. We gave up on trying to follow who was who in the government or the party. The party targeted especially its Social Democrat wing, but after a while suspicion ran so rampant that fellow faithful communists also fell victim to the madness. The deportation of those deemed "class enemies" and reactionaries that started in 1949 escalated, until by mid-1953 over 44,000 people from Budapest and a few other larger cities were interned in about hundred forced labor camps.

The newspapers and radio kept the slogan "Increase vigilance!" in the forefront. Universities and secondary schools appealed to young people's idealism, convincing them that their vigilance was needed, that they were helping to create and protect a system of justice, and a better world for all. But to achieve that dream, they had to eliminate evil conspirators, by denouncing all critics of the system. Brothers turned in brothers, children turned in parents, and friends betrayed each other.

Nobody needed to reward the people who denounced others. They were convinced of the righteousness of the cause (or bore a personal grudge against the person they denounced). One of my mother's English students, a senior in high school, made an ironic remark to a good buddy, with whom he had been studying and playing soccer for a couple of years, about the blatant propaganda he had read in the paper that day. A couple of days later the principal interrogated him about his family, his beliefs, his activities outside school. He truly considered himself a communist, yet he was terrified, afraid of what would happen to him and maybe to his parents. Nothing drastic happened, but the incident was noted in his record and for five years his application to the university was denied. Finally in 1958 he was admitted to the engineering school.

In a similar situation, our physician and neighbor had a dinner with three other doctors and their spouses at his home. He felt comfortable and secure, among friends, and made some critical remarks about how hard it was to get butter, wondering if Hungarian butter was being diverted to the Soviet Union. A few days later he was arrested. His family did not find out where he had been taken for several years. Only in 1959 was he let go, too old and broken to resume practicing medicine.

Rumors of incidents like these were rampant. Many people had friends or family who had been arrested, deported, or fired. It kept most people quiet, making themselves as invisible as possible. The paranoia of the higher echelons of the party permeated down to all of us.

The regime kept reducing the size of private property

that an individual was allowed to hold, and finally they nationalized small businesses. Ironically, they didn't have people who could run them. My mother's cousin Mariska had opened a lingerie shop, making corsets and bras. One day in 1950 two men with briefcases entered the store and demanded an inventory and the cash from the register, declaring the store government property. The next day they summoned cousin Mariska and offered her the job of manager of her former store.

The government took control of all business, large and small, at least officially. Plenty of small under-the-counter business continued on an individual scale, despite the danger of being caught. But nationally, after the establishment of the Council for Mutual Economic Assistance, commercial dealings occurred mainly among the Iron Curtain countries, and the USSR became Hungary's major trading partner. Its economic vulnerability was aggravated by the fact that the forint was not convertible to Western currency.

Although the peasants who were forced into collectives had at least access to machinery, they had to grow what the Central Planning Office and its "Three Year Plan" demanded and sell their crops and meat to the state, at state-determined prices. Who could blame the farmers for selling what they could on the side to black-marketeers?

My friend Loránt's fearless mother bought and sold in the black market just about anything that she could get her hands on. When the local police caught her, she had plenty to bribe them with. However, when it was the state police who on a tip searched her house and caught her red-handed, she spent over a year in jail while Loránt, whose father had been killed in the war, was sent to an orphanage. When she got out of prison, she started right up again. It was too tempting not to since she had all the connections, and whatever jobs she could get wouldn't support her and Loránt. But Loránt paid a heavy emotional price for being dumped in an orphanage at age five, thinking that his mother had abandoned him.

Dealing in the black market was just one of the sins that was labeled reactionary. Reactionary became the label for all that the system considered a danger to its success. The party and government leadership became obsessed with purifying every place of possible reactionary elements (those who had owned businesses, who had been government functionaries, who were able to receive an education under the old system, or who were not clearly committed to the system), no matter how experience-poor it left many businesses and organizations and, above all, the government bureaucracy itself. For the most part this was not rational; there were many, many well trained professionals and educated intellectuals who wholeheartedly embraced the communist ideals yet they were barred from places where they were sorely needed.

On the other hand, people propelled to the top were blinded by a slogan-driven, goal-driven fanaticism about creating a showcase of workers' paradise, fueled sometimes by envy and resentment of those who had had more advantages in the past. Some exceptions did slip in, however. Before the war my friend Alex's dad had been a young but highly placed analyst with the National Bank, an expert in foreign trade. Although his father (Alex's grandfather) had been a newspaper editor, part of the old intelligentsia, and he himself had received a superior education, he stayed in his job because he was pretty much indispensable. He was not only kept on but given all kinds of privileges, like a large apartment and access to food and goods mostly reserved for the party elite.

The affluence of the party elite was the exception to the egalitarian poverty shared by most. They did not flaunt their affluence, however. They drove or were driven in state-owned cars that were black and looked all the same. There were rumors of special stores where everything was available, where party officials shopped but if someone actually had seen such a store, they would be too afraid to say so loudly. Yet the discrepancies between the ideals they preached, the avowals of equality, the sacrifices they asked for and what the population saw or surmised was their lifestyle, contributed to the disillusionment and cynicism building in the many idealists who joined the Communist Party in the early days of 1945-46. What disillusioned people most, however, was the awareness that Moscow called the shots, the obvious political dirty tricks of the party, and the fanaticism of the hatred toward the "old" elements, toward anyone who had something or was educated before the war. The ideals and promises of communism, of a world where it was "to each according to his need, and from each according to his ability," became corrupted and betrayed. Yet there were also plenty of true believers who were willing to overlook the excesses and ascribe them to growing pains.

The system also made honest efforts to deliver on its

promises, in the form of free schools, free medical care, jobs for all, and a roof over everyone's head. But it was stymied by a colossal lack of resources. Free schools needed more teachers than the country had after Catholic schools were abolished. Medical knowledge was not up-to-date, medicine was scarce and facilities run down, and the country was cut off from the medical advances achieved in the West.

Everyone was given a job, but talent, education, or suitability were not the principal determinants of what job one got. The jobs often did not match the employees' abilities and managerial jobs were given only to those who had a lower-class background. On the plus side, the government included with most jobs a warm midday meal (a simple legume stew or pasta dish, sometimes flavored with a trace of meat) as well as free daycare. Food was scarce, so this meal was of no small importance. Free daycare allowed the women, so many of whom had lost their husbands in the war, to work. It also gave a needed boost to the workforce and was an opportunity to show the people that the system was delivering equality for women and liberating them from "the servitude of housekeeping." This was clearly propaganda, but given the scarce food, scarce cleaning supplies, scarce heating, no refrigerator, and no hot water heater, keeping house was no joy.

Every family was given at least a room to live in, even though the housing shortage was tremendous. The district councils owned all apartment buildings (after nationalizing them), but were not given the money to maintain them much less fix them up, and repair the bullet holes, wrecked elevator shafts, and so on. Rents were minimal, almost token, so everybody could afford them, but low rents didn't allow any capital for maintenance. The councils' way of providing a room for all was to assign people arbitrarily to share the apartments of others. This outraged those with apartments (though they were afraid to voice it), but made those who would have had no place otherwise more likely to support the system.

The hotels along Lake Balaton, the beautiful huge lake (about 50 miles long) in western Hungary, were converted into resorts for large government concerns, who sent their workers there for two to three weeks of free vacations as a reward for good work. Before the war no simple worker could afford such a holiday.

Adding it all up, education, medical care, jobs, housing, many people's standard of living fell, but many other people lived better than they or their parents ever had. Communism did become in a way (excluding the party officials) the social leveler it promised to be. Yet not all whose lives had been improved became ardent communists. The population had always been and still was deeply religious (about 50% Catholic and 45% Protestant). The anti-religious propaganda, the pressure against participating in religious services, and the persecution of the church hierarchy gave ample reason for many people to distrust the regime, despite the fact that it clearly improved their lot.

Although there had never been an official state religion, the Christian churches had exerted a deep influence on the government. The party clearly wanted to change that. Communism was, in fact, an evangelical religion looking for converts, and it did not brook competition.

The government could not quite abolish the churches, so they tolerated them under the condition that the churches sign an official agreement that they would "support the political system of the Hungarian People's Republic." The Hungarian Catholic church at first would not sign such an agreement. Its primate, Cardinal Mindszenty, had already been tried and put under house arrest for resisting party dictates, but after further prosecution of the church hierarchy as well as promises, the Catholic bishops finally succumbed. The Calvinists and Lutherans had done so earlier. Most religious orders were abolished and priests were forbidden to preach against communism, effectively silencing a potentially powerful voice that would influence people.

Church attendance was noted by the omnipresent eyes of the local party council and was expressly frowned upon. But the churches were by no means empty. Since the regime couldn't afford to expressly forbid church attendance, many working class or peasant families who had a somewhat more secure standing continued to attend. People whose past or family history was not politically correct, usually did not want to risk another black mark by their name and stopped going to church or, like my mother, traveled long distances to go to church in neighborhoods where they were not likely to be known.

Some religious holidays were no longer acknowledged; the major ones, which the government was wise enough to know they could not stop the people from celebrating, were renamed. Christmas, for example, became the pine-tree festival. But this was a thin artifice, and in practice there were few families where the children were not taught that it was little Jesus who brought the presents. (In Hungary St. Nicholas, that is, Santa Claus, brought presents on December 5, and it was little Jesus who brought Christmas presents.)

As any religion must, communism had to win the hearts and minds of people. The subordination of individual rights to the welfare of the community, and the equality of all within the community, were the principal dogmas. A massive effort of "redoctrination" through education, media, and the arts started in 1949. High school and university became perfect venues for this effort.

Education became less and less the exploration of diverse thought and more and more an opportunity for instilling "correct" views of all subjects, but especially history, philosophy, sociology. Russian was taught from the fourth elementary grade on. Even science was torqued: school textbooks credited the Soviets with almost all invention and discovery. It remained for the parents to balance this education, if they dared, or at least instill a healthy skepticism. But the skepticism itself had a corroding effect—after a while it became difficult to believe anything one heard or read. I think we all became lifelong skeptics—I know I did.

The regime tried to control the informal gathering of people. Coffee houses and other opportunities for unrestricted conversation were frowned upon and closed down. Instead, institutes of adult education and culture centers proliferated. Reading and discussion of politics, economics, and history were aimed to indoctrinate those not previously exposed and redoctrinate previously educated people.

Theatre and movies served the same purpose. Dances and entertainment occurred under the watchful eyes of the neighborhood party organization.

For the younger people (over sixteen) there was the Alliance of Working Youth, heavy on "preparing our youth to take their rightful place in the struggle for communism." Destiny, responsibility, and the greater good over personal convenience was stressed, and thinking about these ideals had to fit narrow channels of correctness. Belonging to the Alliance helped avoid risking being labeled a "reactionary." The younger children were organized into "pioneer brigades," the slogan of which was "Forward." Wearing the red kerchief of a pioneer was invested with a sense of responsibility and mission for the future. Skeptic that I was, I was still proud to wear one. What twelve-year-old wouldn't aspire to make the world a better place?

As part of the "education of the masses" the government made books widely available. Libraries proliferated and paperbacks cost almost nothing. The selection, of course, was bent toward the correct ideology, and books, movies, and plays were published or given space and support according to their "educational" value, which was shorthand for showcasing the heroism of the working class or of those fighting for the working class, or showing the evil of the "imperialist exploiters." Subtlety was banished, to create what felt like parody to the more sophisticated population. But in reality this education was largely aimed at the workers and the peasants, at those who had no opportunities in previous regimes and who had much less reason to be skeptical. Hungarian classics, especially historical novels that glorified

Hungarian heroism, were also widely available, and young people loved them, myself included. Painters and sculptors, such as my Aunt Trudi and Uncle Miklós, were commissioned to produce pieces of social realism. They chafed at being told what to create, but were they not to accept it, they would have starved or been severely punished. So they created beautiful murals of workers at manual labor and paintings of workers at study.

The newspapers were ubiquitous vehicles of propaganda. *Szabad Nép* (Free People), the daily of the Hungarian Workers Party, had the largest circulation. Its rhetoric was blatant, its language exaggerated, its propaganda mindnumbing. Headlines such as "The Workers Party is faithful to its roots," "The working class is united" were daily fare. A personality cult of the leaders, especially of General Secretary of the party, Rákosi, was rampant. Laudatory and hagiographic articles appeared every day. He was honored as the "wise Father of the Hungarian People" and "our Party's master thinker." Telegrams from communist leaders from other countries, congratulating him for this and that, appeared prominently. It was repeatedly emphasized that while there were imperialistic, enemy governments in the world, the *people* everywhere were with us. There were frequently exhortative and celebratory banners above the masthead, such as

"Let the eternal brotherly love of the
Hungarian and Soviet peoples flourish!"
"Long Live Comrade Mathias Rákosi, our
people's and our party's wise leader and teacher!"

"Long Live the great Stalin, freedom's passionate standard bearer and the Hungarian
people's true friend!"

The personality cult extended beyond the papers to
books and plays written about Hungarian and Soviet leaders, men who had factories, schools, and streets named
after them. It was mandatory to display photos of Rákosi
and Stalin not only in all government offices but in every
schoolroom and store. Busts and huge statues of communist leaders and of heroic soldiers and workers appeared in
parks and plazas.

Egalitarianism was stressed everywhere. Besides being
a communist tenet, equality had great appeal in a country
barely awoken from being a feudal kingdom mostly full
of very poor people. Not only was there little disparity in
pay for all kinds of work but great emphasis was placed on
egalitarian address. Before the war it was not uncommon
to pile on the titles. One could be addressed as "Honorable
Doctor Director Mr. Smith." Now everyone became "comrade" (peer, belonging to the same cadre). The Hungarian
word for "comrade," was "elvtárs," which literally meant
"partner sharing the same principles." No deference—at
least in theory—was given to anyone.

Scarcity, as well as communism, became a great equal-
izer. Although the high party echelon and a few indispensable experts in science and finance had nice homes and
all the food they wanted, this was not generally known
at the time. We mostly thought everyone was in the same
boat, bearing the same hardships, which made it easier to

tolerate the scarcities. The difference between the salary of a skilled laborer or office worker and that of the project manager or doctor was no more than 50 percent. Extra pay was given for dangerous work. Our neighbor, Mr. Eszto, a mining engineer, received a salary and a "danger compensation," which increased his income by almost half. All in all, the general standard of living, which was not high in 1949, when the communists took over, was twenty percent lower by 1953. If people were discontent, they didn't dare to voice their unhappiness.

Food rationing stopped in 1949 but had to be reintroduced in 1951. Flour, sugar, bread, fat, meat, and soap, among others, were items only available by ration coupons or on the black market. Some people made a good living dealing in the black market but many ended up in jail. The buyer, if caught, was also jailed—an extreme price to pay for an extra few kilograms of meat. Rumor had it that the best meats and grains were sent to the Soviet Union. Likely as that was, the lack of success of collectivization had a great deal to do with food shortages. The government put farmers under enormous pressure to collectivize as well as to increase production. They were penalized with heavy taxes and harassed in many ways. Yet many resisted. The regime needed an excuse, so the newspaper reported that the reactionary peasants were hoarding food and keeping the city starving. At the same time the powers-to-be tried to reassure the urban population with headlines such as "580 new families entered the production collectives in the Karcag region" appeared daily to reassure people in the cities. Despite exhortations such as "Working farmers! Sow every square foot of land by May 1!" people left farming by the thousands, and while there was widespread hunger in the capital, thousands of acres lay fallow.

Pressured by the Soviet Union, there was a huge economic emphasis on heavy industry and weapons production. Competition between mines, foundries, and factories, and stories of production goals completed before deadline always got a lot of press. The workers, whose government this was supposed to be, were handed back-breaking personal quotas of production. Competition between workers for the highest production was fomented by any means available, both carrot and stick. Empty promises about increased agriculture and consumer goods production multiplied, but hardly any resources were directed that way.

Hungary had never experienced what life under a western-style democracy might be and had just lived through the experience of what fascism and hate can produce. So many people, almost half of the population in the beginning, believed that communism gave real promise for a better life, human dignity, and peace. But the continued heavy hand of the Soviet Union, the fear and scarcity, the system's punitive paranoia and need to control, and its inability to deliver an acceptable standard of living led to widespread disillusionment. The continued, though not very visible, presence of the Soviet Army fueled an underground reservoir of resentment and hatred. Even faithful communists resented the Soviet influence and presence. Yet there were those whose faith never wavered, like my cousin Ancsa. From volunteering to clean up rubble in 1945 at age 17, she volunteered for the army and through the army became educated as a doctor. She ignored all the contradictions, all that was wrong, and hung on to the ideals, waiting always for their more perfect fulfillment.

For most people, however, the fear, the internments and people disappearing, the rumors about food being shipped to the Soviet Union while there was hunger in Budapest, as well as rumors about the party elite living better than the rest of us, undermined our belief that the promise of communism would be ever fulfilled. Despair, punctuated by underground humor, covered the country. Then Stalin died and a ray of hope was kindled in people's optimistc hearts.

Taking Over

March 5, 1953, is a day not many Hungarians have forgotten. I was not quite nine but understood that Stalin's death was important, that it held promise for us. At school we were told the fact without commentary, but the news buzzed. I went home after school with my girlfriend Iby, who lived in a small three-storey apartment house with a flat roof. We got hold of some chalk and wrote the date in huge letters on the roof, fantasizing that airplanes flying over would see it. How did we dare? The years of fear and disappearings we witnessed weren't lost on us. I'll never forget the feeling of terror running through my mother to me as we saw the security police's gray car stop at our house. Or the admonitions of "Don't ever repeat what you hear;" "Be careful what you say or we might be taken away to prison." Yet the impulse to make a statement was stronger.

As the weeks and months passed, rumors spread of a power struggle in Moscow. Quiet talk abounded, people trying to guess what would happen in Hungary. Finally in June the radio announced that we had a new prime minister: Imre Nagy. I listened curiously to the speculation in the building and around the neighborhood about who he was and what this change might mean, and the main thread I picked up was optimism, a surging feeling of hope, an almost audible whoosh, as if the country were letting out its collective breath. What amazed me most was that people openly speculated, something I had never experienced. We listened on the radio of the Gerleis' apartment to Nagy's first speech, which promised reforms. Later in the evening Uncle Réfi told us that after the speech there were impromptu parties in some neighborhoods, and I could see smiles—something very unusual—and a new, lighter step as people passed each other on the street.

Some expressed caution, saying, "Wait, this may not last." Others worried out loud, "Don't say too much, if there is a crack down again, you'll be taken away."

But the good news kept flowing, the authority of the security police was being curtailed and the internment camps were closing. Our friends, the Selendis came back to Budapest broken, aged twenty years instead of four, but alive. Mother's friend Baroness Francesca came back too, with cracked hands and a prematurely lined face, but with the smile I remembered.

All this excitement made up for how boring third grade was. The discipline was military: we had to sit on our benches with our hands behind our backs, allowed only to use the right one to write or to raise in order to answer a question. But that was fine with me, as there was enough chaos in the rest of my life. I was a good enough kid that I earned the status of Young Pioneer and the symbolic red kerchief to wear around my neck. Fortunately no special expressions of allegiance to communism were required—it was assumed, just as it was assumed that teachers and parents alike were raising us to be good communists. And if it wasn't so, mostly by this time no one wanted to find out. In practice I don't believe that too many parents actually inculcated communist ideals into their children, because by 1953 not too many believed in them. Nor did many teachers truly believe, and we sensed that behind their words. But while dismissing the red kerchief, my mother was pleased that I was a good student. She was too tired to take much interest in what I was learning or doing as long as I stayed out of trouble.

We were taught to read music and sing. Reading music was like having another language and I loved it, but I couldn't carry a tune and my classmates laughed at me. I thrilled to just touch the shiny, cool, black and white keys of our upright piano and tried to bring out melodies I knew. Often I begged my mother to play, but she always said no or replied that it would be too sad for her. Instead her face grew dreamy as she retold the story of her big romance and how she was supposed to have been a concert pianist, which I didn't mind because I was always ready to be transported to that alluring past.

Our family had been part of Jewish upper middle class social life in Budapest because my grandfather held a high position in a bank. Their mansion on Keleti Károly Street had beautiful furniture and a grand piano. Music was an important accomplishment in their social circle and her

*My mother on the left, Grandmami next to her,
Grandmami's youngest sister, and Aunt Trudi on the right,
in the family mansion in mid 1930s.*

oldest sister, Mila, had a beautiful voice and took advanced singing lessons. Also musical, my mother took piano lessons from better and better teachers. As was the custom, the family held afternoon salons where family members and invited guests gave musical recitals, discussed literature, and exchanged witty commentary and gossip. They also gave dinner parties and musical soirees, where she or her sister Mila performed and many of the invited people, some known musicians, also performed. The consensus among family and friends was that my mother was headed to be a concert pianist. At one of the salons a promising young Russian pianist, Boris, was a guest. He was considered a child genius and was studying piano with the best Budapest had to offer, at the Franz Liszt Academy of

Music, under an American stipend. Sparks flew between my nineteen-year-old mother and twenty-year-old Boris. They started to go to concerts together and for strolls in the Buda hills, talking about music and the poetry of Byron. They fell more and more deeply in love.

However, a twenty-year-old husband was not what her parents had in mind for her. They had already been disappointed with the marriages of their two oldest, and they felt that the standing and wealth of the family at least should bring what they considered an appropriate husband for their youngest. Boris was hoping to go to America to make his name in the music world, a plan too uncertain for the family, and besides, they did not want young Marianne to leave them to live on the other side of the Atlantic. They pressured her to see him less and to see her more well-heeled suitors more. But the sparks had become flames and the pair found clandestine ways to meet, the secrecy fueling the passion of these two romantics. Yet it wasn't to be; her parents were adamant. My mother, having seen how her oldest sister's husband (whom she married against her parents wishes) was ostracized by the family, didn't have the courage to defy them. Boris received his diploma and left to join his mother in America, and although the lovers exchanged promises and passionate letters for a while, Boris found a new life and—ironically—became famous conducting and staging operas and being a commentator for the New York Metropolitan Opera broadcasts.

To make matters much worse, as my mother started to perform publicly she found herself paralyzed by stage fright when she played to larger audiences. She broke down, saying she had lost both her loves at once, and decided never to play again.

Mother laid her hopes in my musical talent and sent me to a wispy old lady two streets away for piano lessons. But soon it became clear that while I might learn to play, I wouldn't be any good, much less star material, and the lessons stopped. After that she dismissed my wanting to sing or learn to play with "You have your Father's tin ear."

Early in 1953 Mother took me to Aunt Herta for catechism lessons so I could take my first Communion. She didn't want to risk sending me to the church opposite our house to a catechism class, where people watching would know that we were religious, which could still jeopardize her job. Herta was a lay religious, another Jew who embraced Catholicism not just for survival but out of deep belief. She was a distant relative, about 60 years old, kindly and vague. I disliked going to her because she lived in one of the huge apartment houses in Pest that was partly in ruins, bombed out during the war. The elevator shaft with its crushed metal cage to me was a menacing, grotesquely twisted rusted iron giant. I was frightened to walk up the dim, partly open staircase next to it. The ghosts of war lived there.

The catechism itself I liked. I liked to memorize, and the simple answers promised a world of order and of certainty. The double secrecy, however, made me confused and uneasy: we had to hide that we were Jewish, we had to hide that we were Catholic. How could we be both Jews and Catholic? In front of whom did I have to hide what? But even in my confusion I knew with certainty that being Jewish was much worse and it was by far the deeper secret.

Around Easter, shortly after that pivotal March 5 when Stalin died, I had my first Communion in Herta's faraway church on the outskirts of Pest. Father Galambos, the parish priest, was a round and bald man with a kind smile. I was nine, the only one taking my first Communion that day. As I knelt near the altar all by myself and participated in the Mass, the flickering candles illuminating the gold tabernacle on the white altar, the smell of incense rising and then the feel of the Host on my tongue, I felt truly transformed. In a way, it was the day I accepted our situation, accepted that I was in some way responsible for my mother, accepted that I needed to "take over." Without quite understanding, I started doing just that.

Between her teaching and her regular job at the National Translation Bureau Mother was working 16-hour days, so she was hardly able to deal with anything beyond that. I learned to cook a few simple dishes—there were no ingredients for anything fancy, anyway. A little lard, onions, potatoes, and paprika made a good meal, and once in a while cooked with a little sausage it was especially good. Vegetable soups, flour dumplings, pinto bean soup, and lentils became the staples of my repertoire. When there was nothing at home and no money, I made soup with a roux of lard and flour, added cumin seeds and water and boiled it.

Slowly food became more available. No longer

compulsory after the Nagy reforms, collective farms dwindled and the government allowed farmers to cultivate larger private plots. Meat, eggs, and vegetables started to appear more predictably and more abundantly in the state-run grocery stores and in the newly allowed open market where peasants brought their wares directly. A little shack opened up the hill from us, where a peasant family from the outskirts of Buda brought in vegetables and sometimes eggs. The idea of a dozen eggs was unheard of, but I did buy one or two at a time for over three forints apiece, not a negligible amount. Then I could make dumplings.

At about the same time, a kind of open market started in Pest, where both cooperatives and independent peasants brought their fruits, vegetables, butchered chickens, pork, home made sausages. It was amazing how fast people could grow extra food, once they were not required to hand over all they produced to state stores for state-determined prices. For Budapest, where over ten percent of the population of Hungary lived, this market was heavenly after the scarcity of the previous three years. Aunt Fodi, who still came to help with housework twice a week, sometimes stopped at the new market to shop for food for us. One day she brought some Pick salami, a famous Hungarian brand that had disappeared after the war but had started to appear again. Five decades later I have the taste of that first salami still in my mouth. But food from the market was very expensive, and despite her long hours, Mother's earnings never covered our expenses. She had never developed a sense for managing money, and we had to borrow from friends until the next paycheck almost every month. Frustrated

My beloved house at Csévi Street 3.
The top apartment was ours.

and impatient, she was happy to hand me the money and let me try to do the managing, which made me feel grown up. I may have inherited my father's tin ear but I seemed to have also inherited his head for money and his frugality.

Of course, I wasn't all grown up—I wasn't even ten. I still loved the summer evenings playing tag and hide and seek in the garden with the other kids in the building, doing gymnastics on the iron bars of our fence, playing hopscotch on the front sidewalk, climbing trees and picking the cherries from the yard of friends who lived higher up in the hills, or even stealing a few apples with my friend Anti from a neighbor. Anti explained solemnly that stealing fruit did not count as stealing because it was fruit. I accepted his explanation a little skeptically but eagerly.

The newly available food was a blessing but a hunger that food could not satiate gnawed at me. I dreamed of being part of a real family with parents who where there in the evening and siblings with whom I could play and share my worries. I tried to find a way to include myself in the lives of the other families in the building. The families were friendly and knew each other's business, so when one neighbor was sick, it wasn't unusual for another to cook for that family or take care of their child. But that wasn't the same as really being part of any of them, as belonging.

The Füredis, who lived across from us, both worked and didn't have any children. The Halász family, living directly under us, had a son Peter who was four years older and a son Andrew, three years younger, but they both worked all day and the last thing they wanted to come home to was another child. The Gerleis lived across from them and had a boy, Ferkó, who, like Peter, was four years older than I and whom I adored. But of course at thirteen he was too old to pay attention to a nine-year old although he toler-ated my hanging around him with patient amusement. His mother stayed home and their apartment was always tidy and attractive. Mrs. Gerlei herself was very tidy (and I thought beautiful) and both she and Mr. Gerlei were kind to me. They had a special edition of all Mór Jókai's books, all bound in purple leather, which I coveted, though not as much as the tidy, orderly apartment and life I imagined they had. But they were very private and I felt like a square peg in their lovely round family. The Eszto family, living below the Halászes, always had a lot going on with their five kids, but even though their grandmother and aunt lived with us on the third floor, I never got inside their apartment and guessed that they were crowded enough without a sixth kid. Opposite the Esztos lived the Toth family, also with two kids. Mr. Toth worked for the AVO (State Security Police), and so they kept to themselves and we were wary of them. I mostly hung out with the Réfis, the concierge family, whose son, Anti, was my age. Their lives felt more open and they regarded me affectionately, with an amused tolerance. It was not what I hungered for, but a lot better than nothing. Though I kept dreaming about a perfect family, I knew that these were impossible daydreams and that my mother and I were alone, with my Aunt Trudi and half-sisters one step removed.

Other than my half-sisters, the only family we had was my Uncle Andrew, who was my father's first cousin, and the ob-gyn who delivered me amidst the bombing. He lived alone in Pest, with a housekeeper, in an apartment house on a wide avenue. Being a doctor was a better living than most, and it must have had some privileges as his apartment was large enough for more people but he lived alone. Uncle Andrew was tall (like my father), bald, and had a lame leg. He was always serious but kind and my mother and I both felt sheltered when we visited him. Being with him I felt a little closer to my father. He also usually gave us a bit of money, which embarrassed me; although he always assured us that it was only a loan, all three of us knew that it was otherwise.

Visiting Uncle Andrew also meant going to "the city," as we called the central part of Pest. I loved taking the tram and then walking to his place. As the weather got cooler, vendors lined the wide sidewalks selling hot roasted chestnuts and hot corn on the cob, and I always bought one or the other to warm my hands and my stomach. But even without those treats I relished being in Pest which felt like the real city, bustling with people and activity, unlike our quiet neighborhood in the genteel outskirts of Buda.

In September 1953 I started fourth grade. My teacher must have been around thirty, tall with blond hair flipped around her shoulders and a tight mouth. She took an open dislike to me right away but as I continued to be a good student, she couldn't fault me much. I loved learning math, enjoying its precision and certainty, and having a facility for it balanced a little my embarrassment at my lack of ability in music and sports. But I was restless and the teacher took pleasure in punishing every little infraction, like moving my hand from behind my back when she was talking. Her favorite punishment was to make us stand in the corner for five or ten minutes with our arms extended painfully to the sides, as if being crucified. After my first time in that corner I despised her.

Fourth grade brought other humiliations for I felt awkward and uncoordinated and I also became aware that I was dressed badly. Most of the kids wore hand-me-downs, but some mothers were skilled at alterations and made their clothes look not so bad. My mother didn't have the skill or the time. I just wanted to disappear from the face of the earth when I overheard Mrs. Gerlei say to Mrs. Halász, "What a pity that child has to wear those clothes like that. They look so terrible on her."

I hid in the haven of books. Reading had helped me stay

put when I had to stay home two years before and sit by the lamp to cure my ear infections, and now I discovered the world of literature. I made a habit of going after school to the apartment of Mr. and Mrs. Füredi, who shared the third floor with us. They didn't have any children and never considered that a child's reading ought to be monitored. They liked that I wanted to read and welcomed me as I plopped myself on their couch and picked something from their wall-to-wall, floor-to-ceiling bookcase.

Besides the many wonderful Hungarian writers, just about every well-known work of the world, written in any language, was translated into Hungarian, an amazing endeavor considering that ours was a small nation of about ten million people. I read Charles Dickens and Mark Twain, Karl May, Jules Verne, Alexander Dumas, C. Forester, P.G. Woodhouse, Charles Lamb's Shakespeare stories, and many others. Reading I walked out of my world and into new ones, some enchanting, some as hard as mine. But they weren't mine. I was no pirate, no heroine, no beleaguered prisoner. I entered those worlds as an observer and there was great relief in that.

I read dozens of Hungarian authors, from nineteenth century romantics to gritty twentieth century realists. Reading about the heroic Magyars who fought for 150 years against the Turks who invaded us in 1562 thrilled me, and even more Mór Jókai's novels exalting the Hungarian country noblemen, to whom honor and integrity meant more than life. Those were the ideals I was weaned on, along with my mother's teaching that education obliged us to a life of rectitude and caring for others. I immersed myself in the tales of the principled, heroic behavior and idealism (as well as adventures) of those noble squires. Jókai wrote of a world I longed for. Only years later did I understand that Jókai's goal was to distinguish between the virtuous country squires and the corrupt city folk, extolling the "real" Hungarians versus those who "soiled" themselves in the centers of industry, commerce, and the professions, many of whom were Jews. Indeed, the Hungarian Nazis had loved to quote Jókai to show that Jews were not real Hungarians. There was my inescapable paradox: the heroes I admired and identified with never accepted me as "one of them," as a real Hungarian. Yet I couldn't stop wanting to be one.

I felt that being Jewish was an obstacle to everything I wanted. It was also an obsession with my mother. Not a religion, but an identity. The identity of most everyone we loved. Yet something that brought the hatred of people around us upon us. Mother continued to relive the horrors of the Holocaust. Again and again she would describe hiding on the top floor, kneeling over the laundry basket that held me while the bombs were falling, being afraid to walk on the street with the yellow star. "We could have been shot like a dog and nobody would have cared," she would say. "I couldn't walk my little baby in the park like other mothers. We were like vermin to be exterminated." Stories of how Unce Lajos' friend survived the camps, how Aunt Gizi was shot into the Danube, how her adored cousin Heddy, "the sweetest and most beautiful girl," never came back from Auschwitz. How Uncle Arthur and Aunt Ilka committed suicide by putting their heads in their own gas oven in Vienna when the Germans entered. How the bodies of Jews were used to make soap, the gold crowns yanked from their mouths before they were pushed into the gas chamber, how we Jews were used for medical experiments.

She descended into the black, fearful world where her wounds would never heal, and took me with her. I wondered: Why did we survive? Did we deserve to survive? Being Jewish is a terrible thing and we have to keep it a secret. But there really is no escape—it will happen again and then they'll get us. The horrible suffering. I thought Aunt Ilka and Uncle Arthur were right: it was better to kill yourself first. My dreams were often nightmarish elaborations of Mother's stories, of running and hiding, of being operated on by Dr. Mengele, of being forced to stir the cauldrons where my cousins were boiled to make soap. Her stories were carved into me.

Easter that year added yet one more layer to the nightmare. Having had first Communion the year before, I needed to participate in the liturgy and so I went to the Good Friday service at the church across the street without my mother, who still didn't want to risk it. In terrible pomp we gathered, all images covered with purple cloth, the crowded church dark but for candlelight. The church was so full that I was squeezed into one of the side chapels. It came to the Gospel of the day, where Jesus was brought to Pontius Pilate by the *Jews* who wanted him killed. Even when Pontius Pilate was reluctant, they insisted and finally pronounced the most terrible curse on themselves: "His blood be on us and on our children." I finally understood. I, my family, all Jews *are* those children. We deserved to die. We deserved the Holocaust. The weight of it, the enormity of it, felt like it would crush and kill me right there. I wanted to run, never to return, to get it over with and die. But the church was too crowded, and I couldn't walk out much less run. The kind people (would they be kind if they knew?) thought I sobbed for Jesus and petted me.

After a few days of despair I tried to make sense of being alive and decided it was for atonement. That is why we survived the Holocaust. We Jews, those of us who survived and those to be born, had to be especially good, had to accept all suffering and be kind, had to serve the world. This was a noble mission: I had a purpose in life. And so this Easter experience was shattering but it helped me to accept my Jewish identity, and be able to continue praying and going to church as a Catholic. (How grateful I was many years later when Bible historians demonstrated that the guilt of the Jews was a big lie!)

Neither the realization of tragedy nor the seriousness of being especially good stayed constantly in my ten-year-old head. I still longed to be normal, like others. Summer came and I played in the garden and wandered in the neighborhood. I enjoyed eating the walnuts from the tree my father planted in 1945, especially just before they were really ripe: white and tender and sweet. The walnut tree leaves had a special smell when you crushed them and they also stained your fingers brown. The tree was a bond between Father and me. When it was apricot season, we collected the seeds, crushing the hard shell with a rock and eating the seeds, pretending they were almonds. We used them for baking too. Again that summer, I spent two happy weeks at Lake Balaton.

Sometimes my mother's sister Trudi would invite me to spend the day with her and Miklós, which was a special treat and getting there was part of the fun. I took the bus a few stops to Moszkva Tér (Moscow Square), the hub of many different tram lines and bus lines, and then walked from there. Moszkva Tér was renamed after 1948, as were a multitude of other streets, to honor famous communists, places in the USSR, or old-time freedom fighters. It was always confusing to hear the older people use the prewar names and the new names interchangeably, but we learned both. Under either name, this bustling square, with its throngs of people, the yellow

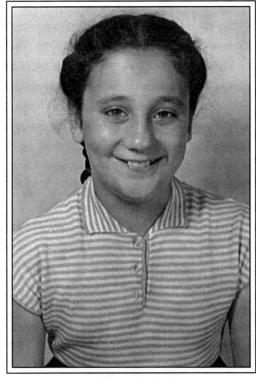

Me at age 10.

trams ringing their bells, and the navy blue and silver buses going in all directions thrilled me.

On Martyrs Street (renamed from Margit Boulevard) the cavernous apartment houses stood, decaying, their original plaster falling off in chunks, the once light stone dirty gray and brown from the smoke of coal-burning stoves. They were forbidding, mysterious, yet calling to me. The buildings had mostly six stories, with eight to twelve apartments on each floor, surrounding a big courtyard. The entrance to the apartments was from the courtyard. Railed walkways ringed each floor, connecting the apartments on each level, like sidewalks up in the air. The entrance to the buildings was often open and I could glance into the courtyard and up. They were worlds onto themselves, those buildings, like villages with their own friendships and feuds, and lots of children everywhere. At the entrance level, facing the street, there were little stores; the bakery, the pharmacy, the fabric store, the eyeglasses place, a window displaying sweaters, a bookstore, and the tabak store selling cigarettes, newspapers, telephone tokens, and candy. It all seemed desirable, exciting.

Trudi lived on the first floor of 58 Martyrs Street, in the same building where she lived before the war on the sixth floor, and where she hid us in 1944. I was always a little afraid to go in the dark entrance and up the small flight of stairs to their door. But once I was in, it was an enchanted world. Their three-room apartment was the most exotic and eccentric place I knew. They had collected old and odd street signs and business signs and had them tacked up in the bathroom, the toilet, the foyer, the kitchen,

*The middle room at Trudi's apartment, jam-packed with
Miklós' painings and Trudi's sculptures.*

and even the living room. Strategically placed, they were
weird and sometimes hilariously incongruous. The middle
of the three rooms was the room they lived in, flanked by
his and her studio. It had tall ebony bookcases by one wall
that looked grand with their glass doors bordered by or-
nate ebony curly-cues and resting on a wider ebony chest.
Although the studio that Miklós and Trudi had before the
war was bombed and they lost much of the art they had
created, the ebony chest and the top of the bookcase was
crowded with Trudi's sculptures, and Miklós's paintings
filled every square inch of wall space, sprinkled with a few
well-chosen old signs. Old, threadbare Persian carpets covered the parquet floor, and the room felt like it had never
been dusted. But the big old stuffed sofa and chair, covered

My beloved Aunt Trudi in the working smock
and necklace she always wore.

in fading brown velvet, were really comfortable and I drank
in the delightful atmosphere.

I was only allowed into Miklós's studio for a minute or
two if I promised to be very quiet. He was always standing in front of his easel, palette in hand, wearing a white
lab coat. He would greet me with some affectionate teasing
comment and turn immediately back to his painting. Trudi
also wore a longish robe, usually striped, and a kerchief tied
at the back of her neck, protecting her brown hair. She was
often covered in clay or plaster of paris dust, but always
wore a necklace, one strand of twisted silver rope. She was
tall and erect and elegant, no matter what she had on.

We had a ritual where I would help her make creamed
spinach, which we would eat with a fried egg on top, and
she would make palacsinta, Hungarian crepes. I carefully
watched how she flipped them in the air but when she let

me try it, I could never get it right. She filled the crepes with sweetened cottage cheese or apricot jam. It was my favorite meal. When it was all ready I got to call Miklós and we all had lunch in the kitchen. Then she and I would lie down on the couch and read, and listen to classical music on the big old radio. Trudi could identify not only the piece, but who was the conductor or soloist on the recording they were playing. (Of course, there were fewer recordings those days.) Other times she told me stories from when she and Mother were young. Stories from a world I could barely imagine. I drank them in, insatiable in my desire for more pieces of my family jigsaw puzzle.

Trudi told me how much she loved her immediate and extended family, but how as a teenager she had felt like she was in a hothouse. She didn't want to study with just her sisters and had insisted on going to a regular school in Budapest for her fifth to eighth grade. She spoke perfect Hungarian although the family always spoke German at home. They all knew English and French too, and the children had a French governess from early on and their father engaged an English teacher as soon as they moved to Hungary. He was convinced that progress was going to come to Hungary from England. Trudi loved art and knew she would become an artist. She studied painting, experimented with sculpting, had fun making furniture out of cardboard and dolls for my mother when she was twelve years old and my mother seven. She also had started smoking when she was eight, climbing out of the window of her room to puff, so her parents wouldn't catch her.

A lover of dancing and exotic clothes, parental disapproval did not stop her from becoming part of the young crowd that filled Budapest's nightclubs every night. The Roaring Twenties were her decade, she told me as she sang old songs like "Tea for Two" and tried to teach me to dance the Charleston. An excellent swimmer and golfer, in her twenties she fell in love with Eugene Kovacs, an Aryan golf pro who shared her zest for life. Over the strident opposition of her parents, they married. But unlike their reaction to the marriage of Mila, their oldest, the parents relented. Gene came to work with his father-in-law on his patents and they all ended up living at the Donner mansion, which was big enough to make for plenty of privacy. Trudi was glad to be close at hand and watch over my mother, who was ultra sensitive and bound to be upset by their father. Like so many paterfamilias at the time, my grandfather, who was known in the outside world as a most affable and calm business partner and leader, was a temperamental and quick-tempered despot at home, a man who brooked no opposition. He also had a delicate stomach and ended up with ulcers. So the family watchword for years had been "Don't upset Papa." My grandmother and mother would quake in their boots, but Trudi could get away with a lot.

Trudi sometimes would tell me these stories on one of our outings. My favorite excursion was to ride the Young

Pioneer Train, run almost entirely by children up to age fourteen. The conductors, engineers, ticket collectors, station masters, and so on were all kids. It was both an educational and a fun project and an honor to be allowed to participate. I never had any desire to work on the train, but loved riding it through the beautiful green hills full of oak and beech trees listening to Trudi, taking a walk from the end station, and getting a special treat, a lángos (hot fried bread with garlic) or a sweet pastry before returning.

At Christmas time my mother loved to decorate a tree and although I had long lost the belief of baby Jesus bringing the Christmas tree and presents, she insisted on the ritual. So she sent me to Trudi's on Christmas Eve day while she decorated and prepared for the evening. With Trudi's help, I made holiday paper, painting pine tree boughs and ornaments on brown paper, and wrapped up something she helped me make or buy for my mother and Móri. Towards the evening we went to Csévi Street and my mother would open the door widely and exclaim: "Come in, come in, see what little Jesus left here!" It was make-believe, but we were touched by its magic, the tree sparkling with real candles, and had a lovely time. Then on Christmas day I would go down to the Réfi's apartment and take a little present to Anti and his sister Marika and admire their tree, which had lots of white gauzy "angel hair" and candy wrapped in different colored paper, the traditional tree decoration in Hungary. Our tree was my mother's work of art, hung with white wreath cookies and other cookies she had baked. Some old ornaments that survived the war also adorned the tree, including a chimney sweep ornament that had been on her oldest sister's first tree and on every tree from 1900, except for 1944. That tree was our family tradition, but I loved equally—sometimes more—the traditional tree of the Réfis.

New Discoveries

Fifth grade opened new horizons: a new school, new friends, new freedoms. The new school (the old one went only to fourth grade) was three tram stops or a half-hour walk away, on Vöröshadsereg (Red Army) Avenue. It was considered sufficiently far that we got monthly tram passes which entitled us to two trips a day, each ride punched by the ticket collector.

The new teacher was "Aunt" Elizabeth. Miss or Mrs. were not titles used, and the all-purpose comrade was fading away, so aunt or uncle were still the eternal titles of respect. Aunt Elizabeth didn't look like an aunt at all. She was young, with tight curly black hair, ramrod straight bearing, and a pockmarked face. She wasn't pretty but she had an enthusiasm, a love of knowledge that swept us up. She was one of the few people I had met who was an unequivocally, totally dedicated communist, even when most idealists had already lost faith. She taught us that all learning can be fun, that the fun was in the challenge of mastering new and interesting things. I loved learning math, grammar, the geography of Europe, the history of Hungary and even Russian. My mind caught on fire and I felt like I suddenly had a place to stand.

One of the girls from my old school who transferred with me was Eta Rácz. Though we weren't especially friendly before, we really clicked now, finding that we thought alike and liked each other's company. Her mother intrigued me too. She was stern and quiet and seemed worn out. I could feel that she too had suffered a lot although I was sure that she wasn't Jewish (not that we would ever talk about that). The family lived in a small, rather dark room with a kitchen and tiny bathroom. Eta had no father either, and as her mother had to work a lot, she bore responsibility for many household chores and for her eight-year old sister. It seemed like they were even poorer than we. Yet she was warm and sunny, optimistic and caring, and always ready to do something and see the fun in it. We taught each other new ways to cook, and often we would cook dinner together at my house or hers. She became my best friend.

Eta's place was right on Vöröshadsereg Avenue, a wide boulevard where our tram to school, number 56, ran. In the mornings I walked a short block from Pasaréti Square to her place so we could go together, but often instead of taking the tram we would trot along the deep ditch that ran parallel to the street, running up and down the steep, asphalt covered sides. The boulevard was flanked on both sides by majestic horse chestnut trees, so other times we walked on the boulevard, collecting chestnuts on the way. The trees had large cone-shaped clusters of white flowers in the summer before the chestnuts would come in their prickly green shells. When we first—very carefully—took them out of the shells, the chestnuts were beautiful, shiny brown.

Besides the fun of walking to school we had a major incentive for not taking the tram: saving one of our rides of the day so we could go wandering around after school. We still would take the tram homeward, but would choose different, farther stops at random and get off and explore. Or we would go to Moszkva Square, the end station, and walk around feeling very grownup, going into the tabak for a candy bar or to the bookstore if we were flush (candy bars were cheap: you could get three of them for the price of one egg). From Moszkva Square we could also pop in to see Trudi, who liked Eta a lot. If we were clever and avoided the ticket collector, we could hop on another tram and explore yet farther. The ticket collector wasn't hard to avoid because the trams were crowded to the gills. During rush-hour it was so packed that people hung on with one hand on the outside door handle and one foot on one of the steps, but that was a bit too scary for us. Sometimes we ended up having to pay for a leg of the trip, but we always had a little money with us and the adventure was worth it.

Before we could seek our tram adventures, there was af- ter-school care. Classes ended at one, followed by a lunch, play, and study period. It wasn't obligatory, but many kids whose parents both worked stayed. Lunch still came in what looked like fifty-liter aluminum milk cans and was usually some kind of legume stew, but more and more often some meat appeared in it too. I was hungry and enjoyed it. The play period was a lot less enjoyable, always some kind of team sport that involved running and catching a ball, two things I was not adept at.

The study period made up for it. True to communist ideals, nobody was finished until everybody was finished, and those of us who were fast were expected to help the others. It was most satisfying to be able to explain a math problem or a grammar question to someone and have them get it. Somehow I could zero in on what hung someone up, what they misunderstood or didn't follow. I felt I had found my calling and decided to become a teacher, a teacher like Aunt Elizabeth who cared for her students and got them to love learning. Eta, too, wanted to be a teacher, one more thing that brought us closer.

My mother also grew increasingly popular as a teacher. One evening a week she taught three 20-year-old boys together who were friends, physics and engineering students at the university. They adored her and she basked in their admiration. It must have brought back for her a little bit the praise and approval that was heaped on her when she had been a young musician. Knowing that she could do something well and successfully was a balm in her otherwise difficult and tiring days. One evening the boys brought over a big glass tube in which different colored lights danced, changing color and movement to the sound of music played. They tried to explain to Mother and me how it worked, obviously proud of their invention and flattered by her interest. One of the boys, Alex, became a lifelong friend of my mother.

Alex invited me to go with his cousin Kati, who was my age, to spend a summer week with his parents in a village near Nyiregyháza, in Northeastern Hungary. I was a true city girl and didn't know what to expect. The outhouse was a shock, full of flies and terrible smells, and we had to go outside to a well to get water. But Alex's parents were welcoming and seemed to like their life, with its beautiful cosmos and roses, sunflowers, and fresh vegetables growing in the garden, not minding the well and outhouse. We picked peas and beans, and fed the chickens and geese. Mrs. Gombos taught me how to make fried chicken and cook sauerkraut Hungarian style. I enjoyed the abundance of food, which was still rare in the city. One afternoon there was a violent thunderstorm and we stood by the open door, watching the huge lightning strikes and shuddering at the deafening noise of the thunder, as the little house itself was hit. The lightning ran through the bedroom and scorched Alex's parents' bed, scaring us but not touching us, and leaving behind a funny acrid smell. Although the countryside was spacious, I felt hemmed in and isolated there and was glad to get back to the city.

At home I ventured farther and farther. The terminal of the number 5 bus was at Pasaréti Square, our little plaza. The low building that curved part-way around the statue of the Virgin Mary, at the center of the plaza, held the terminal office, along with a small café, tabak, and pharmacy. The office had big windows overlooking the buses that pulled in and out of the semi-circle, a few drivers and ticket collectors were always waiting their turn, drinking coffee and smoking. I hung out there as much as I could and became "the mascot of the number 5." The gruff drivers and ticket collectors, in their navy blue uniforms and military-looking

The Chain Bridge with its dancing lights.

caps, became my friends as I discovered they had a soft heart under their stern demeanor. The ticket collectors had big brown leather briefcases hanging from their necks, carrying the tickets, change and their metal punchers to mark the tickets and they wore high laced-up boots to help them stand all day. Many started to let me make the hour-and-half round trip with them, that crossed a large part of Buda, went over the magnificent Chain Bridge, and then deep into Pest, satisfying my wanderlust.

The street names as the ticket collector announced the stops made me wonder about the history of their names. The poets and heroes were clear, but names like bluebell, rabbit, penny, hoer, ray, and so on all must have had stories to tell. The wide squares and tree-lined streets of Buda were appealing, a favorite being Clark Adam Square, named for the British architect of the Chain Bridge, the first bridge to unite Buda and Pest in 1849 and restored to its original design and shape after the war. The center of the square was a round flower garden, with a star made out of red flowers, and as the bus turned around to get onto the bridge, I could look through the old tunnel facing it, leading to an unknown part of Buda that beckoned to me. The bridge entrance was guarded at both sides by two beautiful stone lions. At night, a necklace of lights traced the top of the suspension cables on each side, and danced in reflection in the Danube.

Once on the Pest side, I stared in fascination at the looming buildings and wide boulevards near the Danube, and as the bus went farther, at the gritty, dirty streets of Pest, and the gray, decaying buildings pock-marked by cannon and machine gun fire, some still showing the gaping holes left by the bombs of 1944. It was like descending into the belly of a whale, viewed safely from the bus.

My sister Eva and her son Gábor in 1955, when she was working at the foreign language bookstore and their life was getting easier.

Some Sundays I took the bus to Eva's apartment to play with my nephew, Gábor, who was almost a year older than I. He was no longer the gentle giant of when we were four and five but a large and bossy boy who could be intimidating. Since I was smaller and younger, he delighted in calling me "little aunt." Eva would make my favorite pastry, gooey with apricot jam. Sometimes she would forget that I was her sister and not her daughter and irritate me with lectures on manners, but she was always entertaining, and I loved and admired her. The trip to her apartment was as much fun as the being there. She lived in the center of the city, in Vörösmarty Square, named after a famous Hungarian poet, close to my favorite Váci Street. I took the number 5 bus from home across the Danube to the first stop on the Pest side and walked from there, the street lined with large neoclassic buildings, pausing to look at the Academy of Sciences, that beautiful giant.

Vörösmarty Square was the beginning station of Budapest's pride, the metro, one of the first ones in Europe. It went under the entire People's Republic Avenue (formerly Andrássy Avenue and in the post-communist era again Andrássy Avenue), an impressive boulevard, flanked with palatial neoclassic buildings built in the late 19th century. They were all different, yet harmonious, with an air from a previous time, from my mother's enchanted childhood. Indeed, the very rich (nobility, industrial magnates, and bankers) had lived along this avenue before the war, though not my grandparents, who lived in Buda in a mansion that after the war was subdivided, with another building built where the garden was, and was surrounded by a high fence, so I could barely get a peak at it.

During the war one building, Andrássy Avenue 60, became the Arrow Cross headquarters, a collecting point for Jews. The same building later was made part of the Hungarian security police headquarters, a place clouded by rumors of torture and disappearences. Other handsome buildings on the boulevard were subdivided and converted into offices or used as embassies. I would take the metro to the Heroes' Square and then walk back along the Andrássy Avenue, looking at all those buildings, crossing the street to avoid the block of number 60. Some of the terror had gone out of the country, and these sojourns didn't scare me. Rather, I felt like an explorer and all of Budapest lay before me waiting to be discovered.

Neither Eva nor Mother knew of these excursions; I was simply vague about my timing at both ends. My mother didn't question me, wanting to maintain the pretense that I was always obediently doing what I was supposed to, being where I was supposed to be. That was true most of the time. But if I had to be lonely, without the normal family I dreamed about, at least I also had the freedom that came with the long, solitary hours of my days.

One of the reasons I liked to go to Eva's is that she was a great storyteller and liked to talk about her parents and her childhood. I listened eagerly, always hungry to understand more about my father, hear what she had to say, not just my mother's stories. Some of what Eva recounted had to have been told to her by our father and when I closed my eyes I could almost pretend it was he telling me.

The Fleischl family originated from what today is northern Slovakia. Our grandfather, Izso Fleischl, had been a well-to-do grain merchant and he married Laura Stux, the daughter of a wealthy family from Vienna. Grandmother Laura was a strong woman; she was well educated, intelligent, and ambitious, and at least in later life, not a very nice person. Their first son, our father, Alexander, was born in 1888 and his brother George in 1890. The household was not very religious, although they always kept the High Holidays. Stern and undemonstrative, the parents believed in preparing children for a hard life. They never called their children by a nickname or shown physical affection. Instead, they told the children often that much was expected of them and taught them about family honor and personal honor, about the importance of education and discipline for success. Our father later recalled—with approval—that sometimes his parents would sit down to a good dinner while the boys were sat at a small table and given only bread smeared with lard. This would teach them strength of character, their parents told them. While the boys attended high school, George, who had always been sickly, died of tuberculosis. Heartbroken, the family moved to Budapest to start a new life.

Although young Alexander loved history and literature, he enrolled in the university to study economics. His mother had plans for him to be a successful businessman, and he was an obedient son. But he read a great deal, trying to find his heroes, to discover pointers for life and his place in the larger world. Eva had some of his old books, which were lined with notes in the margins where issues of integrity and meaning appeared. He became a very serious and unromantic young man.

Grandmother Laura was not about to lose her other son, so she pushed our father toward every outdoor activity she could think of. In the early days of the twentieth century the only preventive and possible cure for tuberculosis was clean fresh air, good food, and physical activity that was believed to strengthen the lungs. She didn't have to push him hard, because he had developed a passion for fencing and tennis. He loved the discipline of sports, the sense of personal control and achievement. And he would do anything—almost—that his mother asked, or more often decreed. He idolized her and after her younger son's death, and especially after her husband died, Laura doted on Alexander, though that manifested more in pushing him ahead than in hugging him.

Following Alexander's graduation as an accountant and his landing his first job, his mother arranged for him to marry his first cousin, the beautiful, redheaded Karola Gyenes. Although second and third cousins often married in those days, the marriage of first cousins was not usual. But Laura considered it an ideal match financially and she believed in keeping things in the family. No one asked how Alexander felt, whether he was in love with her or attracted to her, but arranged marriages were common and he agreed. However, shortly after they became engaged, Karola's father went bankrupt and this changed everything in Laura's view, who now wanted to call off the engagement. But Alexander showed for the first time that he had been well taught: there were areas where principle trumped everything, even his obedient adoration of his mother. He had given his word, and of course he'd marry her.

Shortly after their marriage, World War I broke out and Alexander had to leave young pregnant Karola in the stern hands of his mother. He became an officer in the Astro-Hungarian army, which must have suited his love of honor and discipline. Apparently he was well loved by his men, because upon hearing of the birth of his daughter, Eva, the platoon sent a picture book for the baby, with all pictures drawn by the soldiers. When marching into one of the towns in Serbia, he always strictly forbade his soldiers to loot or molest the women. The priest in one of these town, gave him an icon from the church in gratitude, that still hangs on Eva's wall.

After the war, Alexander came home to his new daughter and responsibilities as head of household, something that was taken very seriously in 1920. He found a job as the accountant for a large concern run by a relative, a man whose wife had helped to raise Karola and her sister after their mother died. Nepotism was a matter of course, as the extended family was the backbone and safety net of society. He thrived in his job and new life and was thrilled with the birth of his second daughter, Márta, in 1921. But the job came to an abrupt halt when his boss asked him to cook the books. He refused, outraged, and immediately left the company. Our father not only refused ever to talk to him or his wife again but forbade Karola from doing so as well.

Dishonesty was a much more serious sin than cruelty. Or to be fair, he probably couldn't understand how cruel that was. This stiff-necked uprightness manifested itself similarly when Karola's half-brother, Laci, whom she adored, got into trouble. As a seventeen year old, Laci inherited a fortune. He not only blew it in a year but, trying to recover, forged some papers and only avoided jail because the family stepped in to make good his debts. Laci was forever banned from the house, despite Karola's pleas.

After standing for the CPA exam in the mid-1920s, Alexander went to work for a large concern that manufactured a wide variety of rubber products and rubber parts for machinery that they sold worldwide. Eventually he became the chief financial officer and stayed there until the anti-Jewish laws forced him out.

Already while pregnant with Márta, Karola had started coughing and she grew steadily worse. Against all hope, the family curse of tuberculosis had affected her too. How much emotional or affectionate support our father was able to give his wife, Eva couldn't tell. But his loyalty, his discipline, and his iron will never wavered and he did everything he could to save her. He feared for the children, and the family moved to a house that was sufficiently large for Karola to have one wing and the rest of the family the other. Grandmother Laura came to live with them to help with the children. They also had a young German nanny who became, and remained through the years, a friend to Eva. She helped balance the very strict disciplinarian upbringing by our father and his mother.

It was a difficult life for everybody. Alexander worked

from early in the morning to late in the evening, taking on private clients in addition to his job in order to cover the considerable medical expenses. He sent Karola to sanatoriums high up in the mountains around Vienna that were recommended for their good air and good care. Even when Karola was home, the children were only allowed to wave to her through a glass door. The colossal and unexplainable mistake was that nobody in the family sufficiently explained the danger of contagion to the girls, who grew up feeling that their mother had rejected them. Eva sobbed as she told me how excited she had been upon returning from school one afternoon to find her mother home from the sanatorium. But when she ran in to greet her beloved mom, poor Karola just lifted a hand and shook her head to stop Eva from entering. I suppose had she said anything she would have burst into tears, for which she didn't have the energy.

Laura, who never forgave Karola for marrying Alexander after her father went bankrupt, was not a kind caretaker to her, nor to Eva, who looked like her mother. Little Márta, who resembled Laura's side of the family, was more favored, though in that family favoring didn't mean much. Without Karola's gentle touch, the girls were brought up solely with their father's discipline. They were subjected to a stringent regime of "healthy living" in the hope to avoid tuberculosis. They had to get up at 6:00 every morning, do half an hour of exercises with the window open (even in the dead of winter), take a cold bath regardless of the temperature, and be at the breakfast table fully dressed and ready for school at 7:00 in the morning.

A rebel, Eva had not been a particularly good student, though all her life she loved art and literature. She did not buy into the mystique of discipline and honor, more interested in beautiful clothes and jewelry. But our father, whose motto was "Your adornment should be your brain," sternly disapproved. Although the family had jewelry, the girls were not allowed to wear any. In the ancient Jewish way, born from centuries of experience, jewelry was hoarded and passed down the generations for security, for liquidity to be used in case of danger, pogrom, or having to leave a country. Even patriotic, supposedly assimilated Jews felt they could not break with that particular tradition.

In 1933, the year after Eva graduated from high school, Karola died. Márta was twelve years old. The girls felt devastated but showing grief was frowned upon. Our father redoubled his efforts to keep them healthy. He bought a place in Horány, a pretty little spot on the Danube not far outside Budapest, where his mother and the girls would spend summers. He joined them on weekends when he could get away. Many other Jewish families bought places near each other. There was no segregation, no overt discrimination, but society discreetly grouped itself, whether in Budapest or in Horány, according to whom people felt most comfortable with. Eva loved the place because there were parties, outings, and other families with young people. It was widely acknowledged (though not by our father or grandmother) that she was beautiful and witty, and she was popular with the younger set. Márta, who was younger and cared nothing for clothes or dances, also loved Horány because there she learned to kayak and spent every possible

*My sister Márta where she was the happiest:
on a skiff in the Danube.*

minute on the Danube. Her skiff and camping became her lifelong passions.

Father's interests were not in Horány's society. From early on his joys had been photography, reading, and traveling. As financial officer of the rubber company, he had opportunities to visit clients all over Europe and the Near East and managed to combine these work trips with sightseeing. He and his trusty Rolleiflex found odd beautiful things: old faces, a single flowering branch, a gnarled tree, a windswept vista, a lone cross on the hillside. He complemented his photographs with postcards from the cities he visited and after each trip made an album, adding reflective commentary to the photos and postcards about the art he had seen, the places, and their history.

After Eva passed the difficult final exams at the gymnasium (a much more stringent and comprehensive high school than its American counterpart), Father wanted her to have some work experience, even though he took it for granted that she ultimately would be a wife who would not need a job. He asked one of the divisions at his company to hire her for office work. But he couldn't tolerate even the appearance of impropriety, so unbeknownst to her, he paid her salary out of his own. After all, Eva's inexperienced work might not merit the salary she had to be given. I could hear the outrage in Eva's voice as she recounted this. Things didn't turn out quite as our father planned, though. Eva met young Willie Holzmann at the office and they fell in love. It was acceptable for a nineteen-year-old girl to fall in love but not to have the idea of marrying a boy of the same age, one earning a pittance. Although Willie came from a well-to-do and unobjectionable family (his father had a high position at the renowned Weiss Manfred steel works), Father forbade Eva to see him.

But those in love find a way. Like so many of Budapest's progressives, the Fleischl family deeply admired England, so it was deemed desirable that Eva learn English. Upon a friend's recommendation she was sent to a young woman who had recently gotten an English degree from Oxford and was taking private students. As I already knew when Eva got to this part of the story, that young woman was to become my mother. But I hadn't known (though wasn't surprised to hear) that Eva had quickly twisted the twenty-six year old romantic Marianne around her little finger, and often instead of going to class, Eva and Willie met at her place and went for walks. Eva's eyes filled with tears as she reminisced about their courtship and the romantic outing when he brought along a damask tablecloth, bone china, and a vase of flowers for their picnic and asked her to marry him. After five years of semi-secret faithful courtship, Father finally relented and they married in 1938. It was a wonderful year: they were twenty-four and life was full of promise.

Willie's parents had just built a villa with three apartments in beautiful Rózsadomb (Rose Hill) in Buda. They gave one to Willie and Eva and one to his brother. At the time, this was a very common arrangement among families who could afford it, keeping the generations close to each other. Since Willie's parents had given them a place to live, it was for Eva's family to furnish it. Typical of Father's love of everything Hungarian, he insisted in giving the young couple traditional Hungarian folk furniture—despite Eva's clear preference for something more modern and elegant. Eva could barely tell between her sobs how wonderful and how short lived her life with Willie had been, and then abruptly said, "But you know what happened."

And I did. From hearing the story so many times, I almost felt like I was there when poor Willie was shot before Eva's eyes. Though her strength felt like it rose up from deep down the earth, I couldn't imagine how Eva survived. Her sobs slowly subsided as I tried to comfort her that day.

Then she shook herself like a dog shakes the water off and stood straight up, saying "Let's have a piece of cake."

Eva's and my mother's view of Father were very different from each other. Eva was grateful and admiring of much that Father taught her, and believed that she couldn't have survived without having been toughened up by her upbringing. But she spoke more frequently about her longing for tenderness, about his strictness, about fearing him. Márta never talked much about our father or her upbringing. She didn't like to talk about the past, though sometimes she and Eva would remember something and laugh together. I remember that when our father was alive my sisters would tease him about how soft he had become.

Mother and I pose for a photo
at Miklós' birthday celebration in 1956.

In my mother's stories Father was perfect, and after he died she never dated or brought any man home. She made a shrine of my father's memory and relived their life together, over and over, in great detail. On September 8th they went on a hike and he had asked her to marry him. On the 12th they sat in a cafe in Rózsadomb and that's where she had said "yes." Then they met at the Apostolok restaurant and had an evening of planning. Every September 8th Mother took me on a walk to commemorate that anniversary, then on the 12th to a cafe nearby the one where she accepted his proposal (now destroyed), and to the Apostolok, and on the 28th, their wedding anniversary, we had dinner with Eva and Márta. At first I loved the stories of those important days, but then I became uncomfortable, feeling more and more like a poor substitute for my father.

I relished my life in the spring of 1955. At eleven, I felt more independent, my world became larger, and the atmosphere of fear all around me lifted. That summer, however, the country's hopes and optimism were dashed by Moscow's tightening grip and the ousting of Imre Nagy as prime minister. People gathered to speculate about what would happen and share their unease, but, although there was an atmosphere of caution and worry, the level of fear that prevailed while Stalin was alive did not return. And life in Budapest was steadily easier and more colorful.

On occasion I would go with my mother to Váci Street, the old, elegant shopping street that still held the feel of a different era. The beautiful old buildings had either not been damaged in the bombing and street-to-street fighting or they had been repaired. I especially liked the one at the end of the street with a passageway to the next street and very tall ceilings made of leaded glass. As regulations eased up, artisans were given licenses. The first small stores opened on Váci Street and I could see, even if we couldn't afford to buy, pretty clothes and shoes. Slowly clothes became more colorful and even make-up appeared. It all felt new and exciting. At Váci Street we also would visit Eva, who was hired by the first foreign language bookstore that was allowed to open. As few people spoke foreign languages, her knowledge of English, German, and French made her a shoo-in. Along with a couple of coffee shops, we visited—very rarely—"Mézes Mackó" (Honey Bear), a newly reopened deli that served deviled eggs, little sandwiches, and sweets. Oh, what heaven! And what a change from only a few years before.

My best friend Eta and I in 1957.

At the beginning of sixth grade I received my first pair of glasses. While it was a relief to see so much better, I was also upset because there was only one other girl in my class with glasses. Even so, sixth grade was the best school year I had ever had. Eta remained my true and best friend, with whom I could share my thoughts, with whom I could talk about God and go to pray before the painting of Holy Mary, at the entrance of our church—and who was always game for anything. I enjoyed our easy, natural camaraderie as her upturned, slightly freckled face, wide and generous mouth and bobbing light-brown hair became more familiar to me than my own. Yet we didn't share it all. I sensed some hurt in her that I guessed had to do with her father whom she never mentioned, but I understood that I shouldn't push her, that she would talk about it when she needed to. And then there was the one thing I couldn't talk to her about or to any other of my friends: my Jewish heritage. At all costs that had to be kept secret. My mother also grew to like and respect Eta a lot, and she decided to organize a birthday party for her twelfth birthday. Eta, in turn, loved my mother, appreciated being taken seriously by her and listened to her carefully. It made me feel even more that I had a sister of my own age in her and it did me good to see my mother through her admiring eyes, as I, seeing all her sides, was often irritated by her.

I enjoyed the widening circle of girlfriends. For the first time I felt included and it was delicious. We were a close-knit, egalitarian group; we studied together, we had a good time roaming about, playing, talking about boys, but we were all serious students and had ambitions of high school and university, neither of which was guaranteed to everyone yet. Higher learning was free, but spaces were still limited, and "worker background" rather than merit was still the entry ticket. We nurtured ambitious dreams of success, talked of books, read and wrote poetry, went to the movies. Movies all focused on communist heroes, heroic workers, or historic Hungarian heroes, but they appealed to us nonetheless, despite our street-wise cynicism and what we heard at home about the political situation under communism (now that the fear of being jailed or disappeared for the slightest criticism was gone), despite the patently absurd stuff we read in the newspaper. We believed—perhaps not in communism but in the principles it espoused and failed to live up to. We were young and idealistic and confident that we would put the world right.

For being one of the top students in my class I was invited to the Christmas party (or rather "Pine Tree Festival" party) at the Hungarian Parliament, together with top students from schools all over the city. The Parliament building on the Pest shore of the Danube is a huge, impressive neo-Gothic structure built in the late 1890s. I had delighted in its elegance and beautiful form looking across from the Buda side of the Margit bridge or from Margit Island in the middle of the Danube, and now I was going inside! Excited and a bit scared, dressed in my pioneer uniform of blue skirt, white shirt, and red kerchief, I walked into the building with my teacher Aunt Elizabeth. Thousands of lights sparkling from chandeliers met my eyes as we walked solemnly up the steps of the marble central staircase, covered in the middle by a rich red carpet fastened with gleaming brass runners. The ceiling was so high I could barely see it. It all was grand beyond anything I could have imagined. A Christmas tree towered over us in the big hall filled with delicious treats, and there were speeches I didn't pay much attention to. It was an incongruous place for the seat of a communist government preaching austerity, but of course they didn't build it, just occupied it. I sure didn't care. I felt exhilarated by the beauty and basked in being a part of it all.

I fell in love with the idea of justice and became reckless. One day one of my classmates, Ilona, was publicly criticized in front of the whole school—a very popular form of punishment—for an infraction she said she hadn't committed. But Aunt Katherine didn't believe her. Ilona took it hard. I said, well within the hearing of many, "The hell with Aunt Katherine. We need to do something." I don't know which was worse, to cuss a teacher or to imply that we could protest. Someone told the teacher and as a result I was the next one punished. Not only was I criticized in front of the whole school assembly but was "defrocked" of my red kerchief and young pioneer status. To top it, I could never control my tears when someone raised a voice at me or spoke angrily to me so I cried in front of everybody. So much for my fantasy of being a valiant crusader.

The humiliation of my dressing down brought both disapproval and admiration from my peers. All in all it was a lot easier to get over that incident than to get over losing Andris, my boyfriend from the close-by boys' school. First I dated his friend Attila, but he was too wild and unserious. Andris, with his dark blue eyes and curly black hair, was quiet and sweet, and we could talk for hours when he would call me on the phone or come by the apartment. Sometimes we went to the movies on Martyrs Avenue, near where Trudi lived and held hands. It felt fabulous.

Andris' mother, Aunt Maria, was our homeroom teacher and she tolerated good-naturedly the puppy love of us two 12-year-olds. She did, that is, until the day I brought into the homeroom a photograph of my sister Eva, when she was young. She was so beautiful—something I wasn't—and I wanted to show her off, but when I showed the photograph to Aunt Maria, she exclaimed, "Why, that is Eva Fleischl!" It turned out they had gone to high school together. She didn't say more and I didn't think of it any further, but suddenly Andris stopped calling me or coming to the apartment. I kept calling him, but he offered only vague excuses. Finally, cornered by my insistence, he stopped by one afternoon. He would come no further than the foyer, and would not look into my eyes, but he was able to squeeze out that if I was Eva Fleischl's sister I was Jewish, and his mother had forbidden any more contact.

My acceptability and my belonging had been built on a lie. My friends didn't want the real me. The real me was Jewish, not a true Hungarian, not someone like them. At twelve I had the confirmation of what in a way I had known since I was a tot: being Jewish was a curse that my ancestors had suffered through centuries and even though I escaped dying in the Holocaust, or precisely because I survived, now it was my turn to carry the weight of it. It felt like a heavy weight and I felt crushed, empty, hollowed out. Ironically, maybe some of the other girls were also Jewish, but since they hadn't been found out, they were not about to come forward with that information. I couldn't stand going to the homeroom anymore and for the last couple of months of the school year went home right after classes and became more distant from the other girls. I didn't know whether anyone knew why, but felt that if they did, they wouldn't want anything to do with me either. This way at least it was I who withdrew first. Eta didn't know, I felt sure, because she would have told me. She continued to be my best friend, even more precious to me than before and we decided we were sisters in our soul. Yet I couldn't bring myself to tell her.

Mother identified deeply with my rejection but instead of helping she made it worse. She relived and recounted— again—all the suffering during the Holocaust, confirming that indeed, we Jews didn't belong and never would.

It seemed to me though that she was feeling like she belonged, at least in her little world. Her students surrounded her with admiration, and she was more and more respected and in demand as a translator. At home she happily recounted when she felt she had done a piece of work really well, or when she was praised. When a two-week international conference was being planned in Sofia, Bulgaria, for May 1956, she was named as one of the simultaneous translators from Hungary. This vote of confidence gave her a chance to revisit her birthplace, which she hadn't seen since she had left at age seven. I was old enough to stay alone with Móri, whom I came to love deeply and considered my adopted grandma.

Then Móri got pneumonia again (one of the many

times since her year in prison) and was in the hospital just as my mother needed to leave. What was she going to do? She couldn't disgrace herself by backing out at the last minute. I assured her I would be fine, and she prepared to make the trip. I was excited and a little scared at the prospect of being entirely by myself. My mother had to have a dress made for the conference and new shoes, and that had taken her entire month's pay, so she quickly borrowed 200 forints from our neighbors the Füredis and handed the bills to me to buy food for myself while she was gone. I hated our endless debt and that she never planned ahead, and I right then determined not to spend any of it but make do for each day with lunch at school and go to Trudi's on the weekend. Those were two interminable weeks but I hugged my plan and was proud of my determination.

The evening Mother was supposed to come home, I went to Trudi's and the two of us went to the train station to meet her. The train came but she didn't, so we waited for the midnight train, but she was not on it either. Trudi took me home with her that night, both of us concerned that there was no news. The next day we went again to the train station and Mother breezily alighted from the train, unaware of the mix-up in dates. I remember only relief and a deep relaxation that came over me. But the next morning woke up with a high fever and was paralyzed, unable to move at all. Mother was hysterical that I had contracted polio. When our district doctor came, he thought I was suffering from an emotional shock that would wear off. He was right. In a couple of days I could sit up and eat some chicken soup. I handed her the 200 forints with satisfaction. She shook her head. At that moment we both became aware of the strength of my will.

That summer brought an unexpected visit from Wilfred, a classical music impresario in London with whom my mother had a little romance when studying at Oxford in the late 20s. A telegram came that he was coming to Budapest for the international Liszt piano competition and wanted to spend the week with Mother. His telegram transformed her into a young girl, and she clasped it to her heart, and spoke of him with eyes sparkling and a lilt in her voice. I saw my mother for the first time as a woman with desires and visions of romance. At forty-nine she was still pretty. Her white hair short and carefully waved, her smile diffident, she was slender and had a habit of tilting her head to the side, in an observing, quizzical way which people found charming. There was something regal about her—except when she got mad. Now that I was more grown up she got mad less frequently, though she still had a fearsome temper. Now, with the prospect of Wilfred coming she had a new dress made and bought a purse and gloves. I was excited and a little bewildered at how young she seemed. What would happen to me if Wilfred married my mother? What would it be like to have a step-father? Would we go to England? Although the borders were still tightly locked, it seemed less of an impossibility than it would have just a couple of years before.

The fantasy was premature as Wilfred had married since the last time they could correspond. Correspondence with the West had been dangerous if not impossible in the early 50s and we couldn't even keep in touch with my mother's sister and aunt in the United States, much less with a friend. But the breezes of freedom had blown progressively warmer after 1953, and by 1956 correspondence was free and Hungary was hosting an international music competition honoring one of her native sons. Although not the romantic prospect she had hoped for, Wilfred was handsome and kind and treated Mother to a week of concerts, restaurants, and even dancing. One evening he took both of us for a splendid dinner at his hotel.

As a good-bye present he gave me money for the school trip that was to happen in November, when those of our 7th grade class who could pay for it would go to Prague. It was a trip that never happened, for the revolution broke out in October.

Fresh Air

While I was busy marveling at my expanding universe, trying to hold on during the wild roller coaster ride of acceptance and rejection, of embracing my responsibilities and trying to escape them, I was only peripherally aware of what was going on in the country. I enjoyed the food that became available, the less fearful atmosphere, and a growing color around me, but that wasn't the whole story. The country was going through its own three and a half year long roller coaster ride of political rhetoric, of economic directions and reversals, and most of all of hopes for a better, freer, more humane life awakened and dashed and awakened again.

How did Hungary get from that the release of March 5, 1953 to that fateful day of October 23, 1956? Stalin's death had been like a window opening in a closed-up, dirty room. The fresh breezes stirred the dust wildly and how it would settle again was very unclear.

The power struggle in Moscow following the death of Stalin dragged out, as upper echelons of the Soviet communist party constantly issued and reversed opinions and directives. Slowly a movement emerged away from the central obsession that a showdown with the "war-mongering imperialists," as the West was always referred to, was inevitable and toward the possibility of a peaceful coexistence of power blocs.

For a peaceful coexistence, some of the less hardliners of the Moscow leadership realized they needed some stability and improvement in general well being within the Soviet-bloc countries, without giving up the tight rein they held over them. The situation in Hungary in 1953 worried them. The collectivization was a disaster as far as food production. The continued lack of food, clothing, and housing, and the back-breaking production quotas and harsh conditions that most of the people lived under, could not be sufficiently covered up with reeducation, propaganda encouraging heroic work, and whipping up sentiment against the dangers of imperialism. Although there was no outlet to express the discontent, those who reported to Moscow must have felt the power of the underground rumbling growing.

Rákosi, the number one man in Hungary beginning in 1945, as the Secretary General first of the Hungarian Communist Party and later of the Hungarian Workers Party, was perhaps even more fanatic than the Soviets and just as autocratic. He was convinced that the Stalinists would prevail in the Moscow power struggle and therefore nothing needed to change. Although Moscow issued statements about the need "to right the wrongs of the past" and accused the Stalin era leaders of having committed "crimes against the socialist law," Rákosi would heed no advice and kept pressing the rate of collectivization and the development of heavy industry, even when instructed by Moscow to ease up. Barely three months after Stalin's death the Soviets called him to Moscow and removed him as prime minister. Imre Nagy, an agronomist who had been the Minister of the Interior, was made prime minister. However, Rákosi still retained the most powerful position in Hungary: First Secretary of the Central Committee of the Hungarian Workers Party.

Imre Nagy was trusted because he had been a communist for 40 years and had been jailed as early as 1925 for "communist agitation," and he also had spent time in Moscow. He had grown up in the countryside and was passionately devoted to the land. Even during the years when it was unthinkable to criticize, he had the courage to say that forced collectivization "was the wrong way to build socialism," and paid for it by being expelled from the party leadership for three years.

One reason Imre Nagy was quite acceptable to Moscow as well as the rank and file of the Hungarian Workers Party was that he was not Jewish. The Moscow leadership had always been anti-Semitic and did not like that there was such a high proportion of Jews among the Hungarian party elite. Yet it was the Hungarian Jewish intellectuals and Jews in general who after the experience of the Holocaust had most enthusiastically embraced the ideals of communism, ideals that promised a world where everyone had an equal place regardless of religion or ethnicity. The intellectuals soon became disillusioned with the abuses of power and methods of the party that violated those ideals. Many left, many were prosecuted, many died. But some of those who could not resist the siren call of power and became the leaders of the communist tyranny also were Jews, a fact that helped to fuel a continued anti-Semitism in Hungary.

Prime Minister Nagy, with the approval of the Party Central Committee, promised to institute widespread reforms: to slow the speed of industrialization, to make agricultural cooperatives voluntary, to close internment camps, and to grant amnesty to political prisoners. There would be more tolerance toward religion and more esteem of intellectuals. Nagy was a faithful communist idealist, who believed these were the right aims for a true communist country. But the power struggle in Budapest was no less fierce than the one playing out in Moscow at the same time. Rákosi did not feel bound by his own Central Committee's decrees since he was used to making the rules that the Central Committee rubber-stamped, not to being told what the new directive was. He never ceased to intrigue and undermine.

Nevertheless, things looked promising. People rejoiced wildly when the radio broadcast Nagy's speech announcing reforms. They celebrated in the streets, creating impromptu parties with kegs of beer and barrels of wine. People danced and yelled, "The Rákosi era is over!" That they dared to so openly celebrate and criticize the past showed the resilience of a people well acquainted through the centuries with oppression and calamities from which they rose indomitably each time. They were not looking for the end of communism—not yet anyway—but believed in the honest, thoughtful, quiet delivery of Nagy's speech, affirming socialist ideals in a voice that rang true. They trusted him because he had dared to criticize collectivization.

People had smiles on their faces and a newborn optimism as they affirmed, "He really cares for the working man." Amazing, really, since the newspapers for the last five years had fed the people a steady diet of articles and slogans about how Hungary's government was by the people and for the people. But since all the evidence had been to the contrary, soon virtually no one had believed it. By 1953 Hungary was awash in a hopeless cynicism that people didn't dare to voice but that was palpable. It didn't help that it became more and more widely known that the party leaders, while paying lip service to equality, were shopping at special stores where all food and clothing was abundant, and that they had special, better equipped hospitals, cars with chauffeurs, and so on. Yet, despite the justified cynicism, people had retained a capacity to recognize authenticity in Imre Nagy's speech.

The promised reforms began. The government terminated the autonomy of the AVH (literally the State Security Department, a euphemism for the secret police) and arrested its dreaded head, trying and sentencing him to life behind bars. The population rejoiced at the return of about 750,000 people from prison and internment camps.

Farmers left the collectives in large numbers and started to cultivate their small plots as they wished, bringing to market meat, eggs, and vegetables. Also tiny shops began to appear: a cobbler here, a dressmaker there, a tailor, a leather worker, a hair dresser. Seeing that nobody closed them down, more followed and they mushroomed.

Newspaper editorials, though still quite restrained, began criticizing government actions and pointing out problems that needed to be addressed. Literature started to flourish once again beyond the so-called "realism," which extolled the virtues of the workers and the system. Instead of frequenting government-sponsored cultural centers, people began to go to cafes again, once the great pastime of the Hungarian intelligentsia, and talk to each other. They didn't sit in the cafes openly criticizing the government or communism, but they drank their espressos and talked about their lives, worries, and hopes, without the constraint of the controlled environment of the cultural center. A heavy, suffocating blanket had been lifted—not gone, but at least a few feet off our heads and shoulders. Humor reasserted itself in political cartoons and cabarets. Yet there was also unease in professional and intellectual circles. Many were cautious and cautioning, not trusting that the reforms would last and not knowing who would prevail: the reform-minded Nagy or autocratic Rákosi, whose large portraits, together with those of Lenin and Stalin, still hung in all official buildings and classrooms.

By and large optimism and hope overtook caution. Imre Nagy's popularity soared among both the workers and the intelligentsia, especially after he introduced a bill to gradually democratize the regime by recreating the Popular Front, thus providing a venue for the voice of non-party members. The intellectuals of the party, the writers, journalists, and young scientists who had worked their hearts out to implement so much of the communist agenda but by 1954 could hardly stomach belonging to the party, finally found someone whom they could embrace. They saw a chance to reform the system, purge it from abuses, and make it live up to its ideals.

For whatever reason the Soviets stood by and did not interfere. Then in the summer of 1955, after two years of increasing openness, a sudden change of direction in Moscow allowed the Rákosi group, whom Nagy never tried to oust and who never stopped trying to undermine him, to gain the upper hand again. The admission of the German Federal Republic into NATO in May 1955 had made the Soviets nervous. How was the Soviet Union to respond to the obvious desire of their satellites, the Warsaw Pact countries, for more independence?

Moscow garrisoned Soviet troops in all of the Warsaw Pact countries. In Hungary they were not a heavy-handed, obvious presence, especially not in Budapest. Relatively isolated and unobtrusive, Soviet soldiers were rarely seen in the streets. Yet the knowledge of their existence on Hungarian soil was galling to people, particularly as it was coupled in their minds with the realization that the Soviet Politburo pulled the strings and handed down the directives upon which the Hungarian Central Committee of the Party acted.

On balance, while independence from Moscow was a clear goal, the presence of the Soviet military mostly impacted people's daily lives in that it created so many extra mouths to feed, when food supplies were scarce. People were more focused on the big domestic issues such as the abolition of coercive farming cooperatives and gaining more freedom for farmers, the end of heavy industry production quotas, more light industry that was relevant to daily life, permits for small businesses, better transportation, freer expression, and freer travel.

The hardliners in the Moscow leadership, who were gaining ascendancy, perceived those desires as steps toward independence from Soviet dominance and too threatening. They demanded that the policies of obliterating dissent and rule by fear continue, perhaps not believing that people could embrace communism on its own merits. Returning to their pre-1953 stance, they pressed the satellite countries for faster development of the weapons industry and for squelching any deviance from the party line. Nagy was accused of "slowing the motor of socialist development," and of "pushing the party into the background."

As Moscow flip-flopped, so did the Central Committee of the Hungarian Workers Party. There was no real opinion, at least not one the Central Committee expressed, and no conviction. First they attacked Rákosi's "leftist deviations"; five months later, just as unanimously, they attacked Nagy for "rightist deviations."

With Moscow's always necessary blessing, Nagy was relieved of his position as prime minister in April 1955, to be supplanted by one of the Rákosi troika. Never going halfway, they also forced Nagy out of the Central Committee, and finally out of the party. The price of his remaining a member of the Central Committee would have been a public self-criticism, admitting all of his "errors," which he refused. His popularity was such that they didn't dare to conduct a show trial on trumped-up charges and execute him, as they did with László Rajk in 1949, and by losing his party status he became even more trusted by the people.

The reforms were scrapped and the government reinstated collectivization of farmers and enforced a faster pace in the development of heavy industry. The AVH was given back its unchecked powers. Steps were taken to strangle the beginnings of what had been, if not free speech, at least a freer speech. The newspaper editorial staff was purged and a new wave of arrests of intellectuals accused of being "anti-party and anti-worker,"—watchwords designed to trigger worker antipathy—ensued. But it didn't work. The workers had resonated with the intellectuals' calls over the prior two years for increased national independence, respect, and the elimination of inhumane production quotas.

Once people had breathed fresh air they were not willing to close the window. Opposition within the party and among those expelled earlier spread. Although there were arrests and purges, the system no longer had the stomach for the brutal repression needed for thought control. The masses no longer swallowed the ever-changing party line and promises.

Neither were the intellectuals any longer willing to be silenced. The Petőfi Circle (named after the Hungarian poet who had been one of the leaders of another Hungarian revolution over a hundred years before) circulated thoughtful commentary on the situation and manifestos of the people's aspirations. When it became known that Rákosi was responsible for the false accusations and mock trial of Lászlo Rajk, one of the early idealist communist leaders, people couldn't contain their outrage. The Hungarian Writers'

Association, the Journalists' Association, and university students groups relentlessly criticized the party leadership. They called for the reinstatement of Nagy as prime minister and the continuation of the reforms started under him, reforms that were perceived to have led not only to more freedom of expression but to an improvement in everyday life. No longer could threats and reprisals intimidate the swelling tide of dissent. The intellectuals led, debating principles, and the people largely supported them because after the previous long years of deprivation, a little easing of hardships and a little improvement in the standard of living had represented the promise of much more. To defuse some of the criticism, in June the Soviets replaced Rákosi as the First Secretary of the Workers Party with Ernö Gerö. But he was another hardline Stalinist and the change didn't pacify anybody. The tensions that had been mounting all summer increased to the breaking point after the solemn reburial of Rajk's remains. It was now the point of no return. People's hopes had been raised and they would not be dashed again. If anything, they wanted more and wanted it quicker.

The Central Committee no longer spoke with one voice; as the hardliners and reformists struggled for ascendancy, the government declared and rescinded policies. People in Budapest could feel that there was no clear, unified plan from above. An air of spring emerged, even though it was October, an air of promise and possibilities that fed the public demands for reform.

Revolution

Neither my mother nor I were aware of the extent of political turmoil around us in 1956. The daily paper, to which we paid no attention, carried only the strict party line according to which we were living in a paradise. If there were more radical publications, they did not have wide circulation. When we listened to radio, it was to classical music. Only from my mother's few favorite English students who were studying engineering at the university did we have any inkling of the ferment among students and intellectuals. We worried for the safety of those students, especially Alex, but we were not a political household. We enjoyed the increased lightness and loss of fear in the air, the political jokes circulating, the easier availability of food and things. Only looking back can I see that we were conscious of an unrest, a shifting of ground under our feet.

The university students were the ones who dared to give voice to the grievances and aspirations of the people. The students of Budapest Technical University drew up a list of demands for political reform, the main one being the withdrawal of Russian troops. Then they called for a peaceful march, in solidarity with Gomulka, a reformer who had just been named First Secretary of the Party in Poland, and "our Polish brothers" for October 23rd. The Ministry granted permission for it, but on the morning of the 23rd, when there was a sense that the demonstration could be huge, the Minister of Interior issued a communiqué forbidding it.

In response, masses of students, professors, writers, and journalists met in Budapest's colleges and universities that morning, demanding that "Comrade Nagy be restored to the leadership of the state and the party." In the afternoon, deciding to ignore the withdrawal of their permit, thousands, mostly university people, took to the streets in an orderly march to the Petöfi monument. Petöfi, the young freedom fighter and poet of the Hungarian revolution against the Hapsburgs in 1848 was the perfect symbol and inspiration for this young crowd. At the monument, as someone recited Petöfi's poem clamoring for freedom, the verse that every school child learned by heart, the multitude passionately echoed the refrain "We swear, we swear never again the chains to bear." Emotions ran high as the crowd, growing at every street corner, marched over the Chain Bridge to the Buda side, to the monument of the Polish general Joseph Bem, who had been one of the leaders of the Hungarian Army in the 1848 revolt. The marchers sang the forbidden Hungarian Anthem ("God Bless the Hungarian people....") over and over. People cried, overcome by a feeling of unity and camaraderie after so many years of looking at each other fearfully, thinking "Who will denounce me?" Someone had cut out the hammer and sickle from the middle of the huge Hungarian flag they were carrying. It had

been at least seven years since the people had marched because were inspired to, rather than being required to march
in a function orchestrated by the Communist Party for
some solidarity event for workers, the Soviets, or a troop
review on May 1st. The march acquired a life of its own,
growing like a huge tidal wave, powered by deep emotion.

The crowd, still orderly, marched back to the Parliament
building on the Pest shore of the Danube. As they passed
through the streets, throngs of workers on their way home
at the end of their shift got off at every tram and bus stop,
and joined them. Several hundred student officers from the
military academy also joined in. It was a crowd of about
150,000 who thronged the Kossuth Square, in front of
the Parliament, demanding the appearance of Imre Nagy.
Finally Nagy was fetched. He was living in our quiet neighborhood, quasi exiled, probably unaware of what was happening. When he appeared on the balcony and started ad-
dressing the crowd "Comrades," an uproar silenced him:
"There are no more comrades!" The people who just that
morning demanded the restoration of "*Comrade* Nagy"
had traveled far in a few hours. Now they were reciting the
poem by János Petőfi written for the 1848 revolution.

> Stand up, Hungarians, your country calls.
> The time for now or never falls.
> Are we to live as slaves or free?
> Choose one. This is our destiny!
> By the God of all the Magyars, we swear.
> We swear never again the chains to bear.

The leadership, unprepared and frightened, failed to speak in one voice. After they acquiesced in allowing Nagy to tell the crowd that their demands were justified, they put Radio Budapest on the loudspeaker for the crowd to hear party leader Gerö declare it a barefaced lie that Hungarians wanted to sever their "close and friendly ties with the glorious Soviet Union."

Outraged, much of the crowd marched some distance to the statue of Stalin with the intention of destroying it. They succeeded in toppling the twenty-five-foot metal monument to one of the most hated man of the century by tying it up with steel ropes attached to a tractor, which materialized out of nowhere. Only the boots remained on the pedestal and in triumphant celebration the crowd placed a new Hungarian flag (with the hammer and sickle cut out from the middle) in one of Stalin's boots.

The larger part of the by now inflamed protesters marched to Radio Budapest, determined to have their demands transmitted over the radio. Their arrival was anticipated and they found the doors to the building barred, as the dreaded AVH troops poured into the area and took positions in surrounding buildings. Instead of airing the protesters' demands, the radio kept blaring First Party Secretary Gerö's speech, enraging the protesters further by its clear incomprehension of the national mood. Ironically, Gerö did make some proposals that would have been very welcome a few months earlier but now it was too little too late.

The restless though peaceful crowd must have scared the confused leadership. Or perhaps the AVH, outraged that its seven-year reign of terror might now truly come to an end, lost common sense. Shots rang out from who knows where. Dead and wounded protesters suddenly lay on the pavement and in that instant everything irrevocably shifted. The solidarity march, transformed into protest, became a movement for freedom; it had its martyrs, and was now consecrated. Word spread. Sympathetic workers from the arsenals brought truckloads of light arms for the protesters turned freedom fighters. Policemen and soldiers who did not want to fight against the people gave them their own weapons and the first battle ensued.

The avalanche-like nature of the happening took everyone by surprise, the new freedom fighters as much as the Hungarian government and the Soviets. Though aware of the seriousness of the political unrest in Hungary, the Soviets didn't expect such a huge political earthquake. But they had the troops close by and they acted. Soviet divisions directly subordinate to Moscow, stationed about an hour away from Budapest in Székesfehérvár, began marching toward Budapest around 10 pm with orders to be deployed to secure the strategically and politically important positions of the city (Parliament, the Ministry of Defense, Party Headquarters, the Soviet Embassy, bridges, and so on).

By late that night, our apartment house was abuzz. Mr. Halász had gotten caught in the crowds and did not get home until late, full of confusing stories of what he had seen. And confusion, guessing, and rumors are what we experienced away from the action in the outskirts of Buda for the next weeks. That first night the worried grown-ups forbade us to leave the house. Eta's mother also forbade her to leave but she snuck out to the nearby payphone to call me and we excitedly exchanged the news we had heard. We children were excited and raced up and down, apartment to apartment trying to find out more, carrying the news we gleaned. Finally someone said they had heard that there would be no school tomorrow. That had never happened before, and now we knew something big was afoot. The families in the house held worried discussions. Although things had been feeling freer, the consequences of dissention and criticism could turn dire again with what felt like just the turn of a screw. Tuning in to the radio, we heard only that some traitorous fascists were trying to cause trouble and spread lies against our heroic friends, the Soviets.

People were awakened October 24th by the radio's periodically repeated announcement: "Fascist and reactionary elements have launched an armed attack against our public buildings and against our forces of law and order. In the interest of reestablishing order, all gatherings and demonstrations are forbidden." Then music, and no further information. But underground intelligence, even in that era of very limited communication technology and hardware was fast and effective. Demonstrations similar to the one in Budapest were occurring in university and industrial cities across Hungary.

Ignoring the injunction against gathering, people congregated in the heart of Budapest on the 25th in even larger number than on the 23rd. Soviet troops fired into that crowd gathered in front of the Parliament, killing 55 people. In response, entire garrisons of the Hungarian army,

*Hungarian freedom fighters taking over a Soviet tank and
flying the new Hungarian flag, that is, returning to the
pre-war national coat of arms in the middle.
(From "Hungarian Revolution, 1956" by Ákos Réthly)*

National Guard, and police joined the insurgents, providing them with machine guns and even tanks. The clash had
escalated into a Hungarian-Soviet battle.

Confusion reigned. Those in power didn't want to seem
indecisive so they opted for action, swinging between
granting concessions and digging in their heels. They continued to impose martial law and curfews that they didn't
have the stomach to enforce. Then they named Imre Nagy
premier again. Two days earlier this gesture may have been
sufficient but now it was too late. Nagy was not an inspired
leader. A man of deep convictions, he was a negotiator, not
a visionary. The people who a couple of days earlier only
insisted upon his reinstatement as premier, couldn't trust

Nagy to carry out the reforms they now demanded—or did not trust the system to allow him to do so. The insurgents did not respond to his reinstatement by laying down their arms. The time for patience and for slower, reasoned, negotiated progress seemed to be over. The concessions that were made were like tinder fueling a desire for larger reforms.

For us, the days following October 23rd passed in a blur of excitement and boredom. It was too exciting to just curl up on the couch and lose myself in a different place and time, whether it was with Jules Verne or one of my favorite Hungarian historic novels. Yet there was not much else to do except when we heard a new tidbit and could carry the news further. All the adults were home too. No school, no work, and a curfew with hours that changed every day. We didn't know that people in the inner city were ignoring the curfew, though we heard rumors of fighting. The radio announced that Imre Nagy was named premier and I heard Mr. Eszto and Mrs. Halász commenting that this was a hopeful sign. I liked Mr. Nagy because he lived in a villa on Orso Street, not far from us and once I had seen him on the number 5 bus, my closest brush with real power.

In between short announcements that warned that anybody seen on the street violating the curfew might be shot, the radio played Beethoven's Egmont Overture over and over again like a kind of Chinese water torture. Still, nobody wanted to turn off the radio because we might miss something momentous. We were in suspended animation, collectively holding our breath without knowing what we were waiting for.

There was a chance that had the freedom fighters laid down their arms, ultimately Nagy could have made a difference and avoided much bloodshed and suffering. As the fighting continued, however, with most of the Hungarian military having joined the insurgents, the party Central Committee invoked the Warsaw Pact and asked formally the Soviet troops to restore order. The government-controlled radio station kept spewing its formula that this was a reactionary attack against the people, and issuing threats to the insurgents, "Capitulate or be crushed." Any semblance of normalcy in the city was gone. All traffic was halted. No newspapers were published. People like us, who were not engaged in the fighting or foolhardy enough to go out and gawk, huddled in front of the radio, hoping to find out what was happening.

The rumors continued to fly, almost as if plucked from thin air. Someone said a lot of people had been killed. Then Uncle Réfi came home from the nearby tavern with the news that the entire Hungarian army, batallion after batallion, had joined the movement, and there was a real revolution going on. Mr. Toth, the AVH official who lived in deported Seléndi's apartment on the first floor, had vanished. His wife and children were not part of our group, so even if they knew something, we couldn't find it out. It is not that we disliked the family but we kept our distance out of fear. They must have understood that and they had never tried to be part of the life of the building.

Every day new, dizzyingly confusing and contradictory announcements came over the radio. Nagy's radio address of the 27th promised that at the next session of the

Parliament the government would be reorganized along the lines of a democratic assembly, and that the government would open negotiations with the USSR about national independence and withdrawal of Soviet troops stationed in Hungary. On the heels of that announcement came one of a curfew and the message: "Anybody on the streets faces the risk of being shot."

Nagy in fact promised to accomplish the major demands that the students formulated on October 23rd. But once called upon, he could not stop the Soviet troops who were fighting to squash the revolution nor overcome that moment when the first shots were fired and gave the movement for freedom its martyrs. People ignored the threats. Insurgents—young workers, soldiers, cadets, university students, professors, people from every walk of life—continued to fight. Even children threw Molotov cocktails at tanks. Dozens of burned out tanks littered the streets. The destruction was tremendous and merciless and in the center of the city the death toll mounted. Buildings, barely repaired from the damages of World War II, became mortar-riddled ruins once again. The better equipped and larger Soviet army was winning, and by the end of the week, five days after it all started, the freedom fighters in Budapest held only the huge Kilian barracks.

Ignoring all evidence that the uprising was failing, people mobilized, acting as if the battle of arms had been won. In Budapest and other larger cities worker councils took over factories. National committees and revolutionary committees spontaneously formed in towns and villages throughout the country. Their demands everywhere

*The Killian barracks on October 25th. Insurgents in
the foreground perhaps walking home after a day of fighting.
(Photo by Erich Lessing/Art Resource, NY)*

were similar, including the withdrawal of the Soviet troops,
national sovereignty, and free elections. There was no suggestion of repudiating communism. By and large workers
and peasants wanted to build upon what they had gained
under the ideals of communism, even though in practice so
much hadn't worked.

Ceaseless supportive radio broadcasts from the West
influenced the insurgents to keep on fighting. "The heart
of America goes out to Hungary" was the message from
the US State Department as it reported that the US had
opened discussions with Britain, France, and other friendly
countries about submitting the Hungarian question to the
UN Assembly. The people, naive about the workings of the
West and of the UN, read much more into that statement
than was there. They knew that morality and international

principles of democracy were clearly on their side, so they had reason to be optimistic. What they didn't realize was that the UN was a place to negotiate and bargain and that they would become a pawn in that system.

Politics and fighting worked in tandem. A week after the first shot was fired the Central Committee of the Hungarian Workers Party, the real seat of power in Hungary, met and dissolved itself, acknowledging that the uprising was a popular, democratic movement. In a symbolic gesture of the shift of power from the communist party to the government, Nagy moved his office from the Central Committee building to the nearby Parliament building.

Someone brought the news to our house that the border with Austria, closed tight since 1949, was open. The Russian soldiers who guarded it were gone, the remaining Hungarian border guards were on "freedom's side." But with no train service and no private cars, making the more than 100-mile trek to the border seemed impossible, though many were itching to leave.

Although the fighting continued, it must have been clear to most that the USSR could crush any military revolt and that only a negotiated agreement could work. Nagy, in his element as a principled negotiator, stayed in constant communication and consultation with Soviet envoys in his quest to fulfill the promise of an independent Hungary. The details can be only surmised, but on October 30, a week after the first demonstration, the Soviet envoy declared that the USSR had "complete respect for the sovereignty of each socialist state" and agreed to withdraw its troops and renegotiate its relationship with Hungary.

A jubilant Nagy announced on the radio, to a stunned country, "My Hungarian brothers! I inform you that the evacuation of the Soviet troops... has already started." Radio Miskolc in Northern Hungary confirmed that same evening that the troop movement towards the border was visible.

It was scarcely believable. Excitement. Hope. Confusion. Wariness. We felt it all, adults and children alike, as we sat together listening to the radio in one apartment or another, sharing morsels of gossip that people gathered in their limited forays. I listened, absorbing it, sharing the optimism and the wish for a free Hungary. But I sensed also my mother's unease and understood her unspoken thoughts. What would this change mean for us? Would there be a new wave of anti-Semitism?

As the new government struggled to get established, there was no clear agreement of how far to repudiate the previous system. Nagy never wavered in his allegiance to communism. Most of the other leaders believed in it even as they wanted an independent, Hungarian brand of communism. The military leaders who joined the revolution were communists by conviction. The writers and intellectuals who were at the forefront of the debates that led to October 23rd continued a passionate discussion on how to consolidate the gains of socialism and reform and democratize the government, not to abolish it. There were, of course, those who wanted to go right back to an ultra-Hungarian (one might say fascist) government, and a multitude of people found themselves somewhere in between. Old supporters of the Smallholders Party called for free elections, and Nagy's government agreed to form a representative government.

The news got better every day. The party's newspaper, *Szabad Nép* ("Free People") the paper with the widest circulation, appeared again with a slightly modified name and with the old Hungarian Kossuth banner at the masthead. It saluted "the victory of the young revolutionaries."

On the night of November 1, the streetlights were still not working but thousands of candles from apartment windows illuminated the streets. The next day was All Souls' Day and Budapest was commemorating its fallen heroes of the prior week.

Buses and some trams lines (where the tracks had not been ripped up) started up again and stores opened on the first, just in time as our food supply had dwindled to nothing. In the beginning we had had some sausage that Aunt Fodi had brought and there were plenty of potatoes, but they had given out days before. With no refrigerator and limited space no one thought more than a couple of days ahead; the custom was to buy food daily, most people stopping by the store on their way home from work. So now we got busy standing in line at the grocery store to buy whatever they had, which wasn't much, because the revolution had disrupted deliveries. We heard that peasants had brought up truckloads of food for the freedom fighters and that a convoy from Austria was bringing food and medicine to Budapest, but none of it reached us on the outskirts.

Isolated by living so far out from the inner city, we had little idea of the devastation suffered, the lives lost, the buildings in rubble, the blackened tanks, the torn up

*Overturned tram in the city with graffiti calling for
the Russians to leave and free elections.*

tram lines, and ripped up cobblestones used to build barricades—nor the start of a rampage of revenge. When Mr. Tóth reappeared, begging us to hide him and not turn him in, pointing out that he had never harmed us in any way, we thought it was all nonsense. It was an embarrassing, strange scene. But of course the families in the building assured him (and meant it) that no one would want any harm to come to him or his family.

The next day I understood his fear. As I walked down Kelemen László Street towards the tram, I saw a man hanging, I think from the lamp post, horribly disfigured, in his gray AVH uniform. I heard myself scream and ran home as fast as my legs would carry me, sobbing and vomiting. In books liberated people were always noble and generous. So this was the true face of revenge! It made me hate people, hate humanity. It made me hate being alive.

There was no one to talk to. I understood that the AVH deserved hatred, even decent people couldn't help thinking that the man probably deserved to be hanged. I stuffed my feelings down. The experience robbed me of a trust and hope for humanity that had up to then survived despite my mother's stories of the Holocaust. This was my own personal encounter, in the flesh, and to this day I cannot drive out the image of the hanging man. Later we would hear of many such killings.

As soon as the buses started running again we went into town to check on Trudi and Miklós, who were fine. There was a feverish optimism in the air underlain by wariness. We kept hearing of people heading toward the border, leaving for the West. The newspaper, with its new Kossuth banner that spoke of the momentousness of the change louder than words, announced that a new government had been formed, including representatives of the Smallholders Party. But Radio Free Europe, listened to on short-wave radios more and more openly since 1953, sowed confusion and distrust by characterizing the new government as a "Trojan Horse," inciting for a complete break with communism.

On Friday, November 2nd, Nagy announced Hungary's withdrawal from the Warsaw Pact and its neutrality. The same day factories and offices reopened and it was announced that schools would start up again on Monday. I was very ready to go back and anxious to talk over all the happenings with my classmates. Life seemed to normalize, and had a promise of something better.

Unbeknownst to the population, during the second

week of the revolution much was happening on the diplomatic front. Despite our high hopes, there was no Western pressure on the USSR to withdraw from Hungary. In fact, on October 29th just a few days before the presidential election, the Soviets received reassurance from the Eisenhower Administration that the US would not interfere militarily in Eastern European affairs. The attention of the Western world and the United Nations was not on Hungary but on the Suez Canal. Egyptian leader Gamal Abdel Nasser declared his intention to nationalize the canal, built and owned by France and Great Britain, and in response, British and French troops had occupied key military positions along it. A week-long war ensued, almost concurrently with the Hungarian revolution, and that became the top issue for the UN for the next weeks. The superpowers made a covert deal: the Soviets wouldn't interfere in Suez and the West wouldn't interfere in Hungary.

Thus the USSR got a green light from the Western powers for whatever approach they took to Hungary. It is not likely we will ever know what prompted the Soviets on October 30th to promise the withdrawal of their troops. Perhaps when the Soviet envoy came to Budapest to declare that the USSR had "complete respect for the sovereignty of each socialist state," he represented a true decision made in Moscow. But by the time he returned to Moscow two days later, the winds blew from a different direction, and a new thinking had emerged. If they allowed Hungary to oust the Soviet troops and leave the Warsaw Pact, how could they prevent the Czechs or the Poles from doing the same? It might be the end of the Warsaw Pact. East Germany and

Rumania, the staunchest and most brutal members of the pact, pressured Moscow not to allow Hungary to withdraw. The Soviets had a bigger problem too: if the Warsaw Pact weakened, Soviet republics such as the Baltics and Ukraine, republics that never wholeheartedly embraced the union of the USSR, might start musing about their own independence. Soviet prestige and strength would falter. Thus Hungary could not be allowed to leave the pact.

Not privy to the change of heart in Moscow, for the next few days the country was feverishly organizing itself into a new, multiparty political system, developing economic strategies, and planning for reconstruction. Not surprisingly, given the intense speed of change, some of the initial purity and discipline of the revolution began to fall victim of ambition, greed, and rage. In that first week there had been an unspoken honor system that when windows of stores were broken during the fighting merchandise was left everywhere intact. In the revolution's second week finger pointing, public accusations, and power jockeying started. Criminals together with political prisoners were freed, and looting became widespread. People enraged, remembering their own or others' suffering, revenged themselves by randomly executing a number of security police members. Despite all of that, the general feeling in the country remained one of hope and optimism.

The optimism wasn't universal however; thousands of skeptical Hungarians who did not trust this sudden miracle headed towards the western border to escape to Austria. Their number increased as rumors came from Eastern Hungary that Russian tanks and troops were rolling back in. When questioned by the press, the Soviet Embassy vaguely explained that it was just part of the confusion of withdrawal. At the same time tanks encircled the aerodromes of Budapest and several large cities, and again the Soviet Embassy placated us, this time with a communiqué that the tanks were to ensure safe withdrawal of the sick and wounded and other Soviet personnel. Our wish of liberation was too strong to believe that we had been duped, and Nagy's belief in honor made him credulous as well.

On Sunday morning, November 4, however, we woke up to airplanes flying overhead and the sounds of bombing and shelling. This time living on the outskirts didn't prevent us from knowing something was very wrong. The sounds stirred memories in me from my babyhood that I shouldn't have been able to remember. Yet without a doubt, in my gut I remembered.

The Soviets launched their attack from the air and on the ground. Aptly named "Operation Whirlwind," they quickly disarmed Hungarian garrisons and began attacking pockets of resistance fighters. Wanting to minimize bloodshed in a hopeless situation, the Nagy government called on all to lay down their arms. But the call went unheeded. Freedom fighters attacked the Soviets wherever they could and for two weeks the battle raged square by square, street by street. Unforgivably, Radio Free Europe and the Voice of America kept broadcasting encouragement to the resistance fighters to keep fighting, suggesting that help was on the way, even though they knew otherwise.

We did what people under siege do: hunkered down

and tried to figure out how to survive. We huddled by the radio, twisting the dial this way and that, catching snippets. When the bombing sounded close we went to the cellar. At first it was frightening, but nothing happened close to us, so packs of cards appeared and we kids played canasta most of the day and the night to distract ourselves.

The radio was again in the hands of the new government (how many had we had in the past year?), which everyone feared was really the old government. It was from a radio announcement that we learned that Moscow made János Kádár the head of the "New Hungarian Revolutionary Worker-Peasant Government." The news was met with incredulity. I heard Aunt Fodi telling Mrs. Halász that Kádár was an old-line communist, that he had been jailed by the Rákosi regime, and that he had been a member of Nagy's true revolutionary government. That would make him a good guy. There was palpable bewilderment in our little circle of neighbors: How could he have forgotten the years of torture he suffered, including losing an eye? How could he have turned traitor? My imagination carried me to his torture cell and I couldn't believe that someone like that could be a really bad guy. I believed that all who suffered became better people, that that was the only acceptable reason why there was so much suffering.

Dreadful stories of killings and destruction filtered daily into the neighborhood. The fighting no longer was confined mostly to Pest and freedom fighters were pulling into key positions in Buda. Rumors of a fierce battle going on at Széna Square reached us and we worried nervously about Trudi and Miklós, who lived near there. The noise of shelling was audible all around us, yet we couldn't tell where it was coming from. Like most of our neighbors we were totally out of food. No bread left, not a can of meat or vegetables, no potatoes. And we were also out of coal for the little stove that warmed our room. It was bitter cold.

A wholesale bakery beyond Red Army Avenue, near where Eta lived and the tram to school ran, supplied some of the government grocery stores in the area, including our store on Pasaréti Square. The grocery store was closed, but through the grapevine we found out that the bakery would sell bread directly to people who came during the night when the bread was baked. My mother and I decided to go at about ten in the evening, and by the time we arrived there must have been several hundred people in line. It was a clear, cold, starry night. I had outgrown my shoes and winter coat, so I had on only sandals, a sweater and scarf, and mercifully a pair of knit gloves. Mother left me there to stand in line while she went home to get a bit of rest, and promised to relieve me in about two hours. I hadn't known until then what true teeth-chattering was. The line didn't even start moving until my mother came back after midnight. By then there were also at least a hundred people behind me. I ran toward home as fast as my feet would go, the cold air piercing my lungs. Loud explosions shook the air as I reached our building. The shelling was coming closer. The fear that the breadline had been hit, that my mother was hurt or dead, paralyzed me for a moment, but I had neither the courage nor the strength to run back.

But once in the apartment the fear that she got hurt gnawed my insides instead of hunger until my mother came home triumphantly carrying a two-pound loaf of bread. Everyone got bread that night, we heard, but the bakery had used up all their flour and there would be no more. Shared with Móri, the bread lasted us for at least a couple of days.

The next two days passed uneasily. Mrs. Halász walked around with swollen eyes. Her 17-year-old son had left for the border, hoping to make it through to Austria, and nobody had heard from him yet. The shelling noise continued, sometimes loud and close, keeping us on edge. About ten minutes walk from us there were barracks, still in Hungarian hands as far as we knew, but nobody dared to walk in that direction to find out. We were cold and hungry. We heard that someone farther down Pasaréti Street, in the opposite direction from the barracks, was selling sacks of coal. I found the place easily (there was a line) and managed to get a twenty-pound sack, which warmed me twice, once taking it home and once as it burned. Móri was battling pneumonia again and sleeping in our room next to the stove. We made a small fire in the morning to take the chill off and then spent as much time as we could under blankets.

To the neighborhood's surprise and relief our grocery store at Pasaréti Square opened one morning. Word spread like wildfire and a long line formed immediately as I raced to get in it, hoping Mother would find out where I was and come to relieve me. She did, but not until I stood in the line for a couple of hours. It wasn't raining or sleeting, but the cold was bone-chilling, humid. In my open-toed sandals my toes were numb, as was the rest of me by the time my mother came to relieve me. I went to the apartment to warm up and drink some hot chicory coffee, which was all we had left, before returning to relieve her.

The sound of machine gun fire came closer and closer. Those of us in line figured the Soviets were taking the near-by barracks and I thought of all those young men dying. Nothing seemed worth that. My fear was mingled with my determination to stay in that food line even if they were going to kill us. Confusion, anger, frustration, and numbness covered it all. Between my mother and me, we had stood in line almost six hours by the time truckloads of Soviet soldiers careened into Pasaréti Square. They jumped off the trucks and pointed their machine guns at us, motioning with the barrels for us to leave, yelling "davay, davay" (one of the few Russian words we all knew: "go away"). God knows what possessed the hundred or so people still in line for lard and potatoes, but we stared defiantly and didn't move. The soldiers weren't monsters. We were idiots and their humanity trumped their anger, even though they must have been fed up with the guerilla resistance they had encountered the previous few days. Instead of mowing us all down, they lifted their machine guns and fired into the air. The sound of machine gun fire at ten feet was enough to make us come to our senses. I never looked back but ran the couple of hundred yards to the edge of our lilac hedge where I could dive under and come up into the garden and run up the three flights of stairs. Mother took one look at my convulsive sobbing and hit me hard across the face, stopping the hysterics cold. So I was alive. But all those hours of freezing were for nothing. We still didn't have any food.

I didn't leave the apartment for the rest of the day, and by the next day the soldiers were gone, we presumed into the nearby barracks. The day after that we saw once more a big truck pulling up at the store and the line formed again quickly. This time we got some potatoes and onions and some lard and were jubilant looking forward to a real feast.

A couple of weeks after the Soviets returned to Hungary the fighting in Budapest was over. We heard of sporadic skirmishes in the hills, but that was all. The revolution was dead, rechristened the "counter-revolution" on the radio. The fight for freedom and many of the freedom fighters were dead. Jailings and reprisals started but they didn't stop the widespread strikes and protests, all denounced on the radio and in the paper as the work of fascist elements. We were at the periphery of it all; sad, fearful, and mired in uncertainty as to what would happen next. Although we didn't know it at the time, in Budapest alone the death toll was over 2,700 and the wounded numbered almost 20,000. The new government arrested another 20,000 people and ultimately executed 229, including Imre Nagy.

The country was in an impotent and incredulous rage—toward the Soviets and toward Kádár. How could Kádár have betrayed the movement? It turned out the Soviets whisked him to Moscow on November 1st, having made their decision. In fairness, his only choice if he wanted to live was to say yes, and had he said no, they would have gotten someone else to head up the government who perhaps would have been far worse for the country.

As tram and bus service was partially resumed, we went again to check on Trudi and Miklós. At Széna Square, we could hardly believe our eyes—the beautiful old buildings were riddled with holes and a tank stood at each side of the square, pointing in opposite direction. Trembling turned my legs into rubber. It was a relief to find that Trudi and Miklós had weathered it all, though some days they had slept in the kitchen because the other rooms looked onto Martyrs Avenue where bullets were flying.

After our visit we ventured on to see Eva. At Clark Adam Square, the Buda-side entrance to the Chain Bridge, tanks stood aimed in all directions, and as the bus turned onto the bridge, the open mouth of the tank's gun shaft loomed a foot away from my window and I could look straight down it. All the experiences of the past weeks caught up with me and I started screaming. Mother had to slap me across the face once again, and the people on the bus nodded sympathetically. I don't know whether they felt sorry for me or were sympathetic to my mother for having a difficult child, but nobody said anything.

At Eva's a new shock awaited. On November 3rd our sister Márta had come to Eva's apartment to say goodbye then headed on her motorcycle toward the border. I couldn't believe she had left without saying goodbye to me. I felt like someone punched me in the stomach. My beloved sister, who even though she was 23 years older than I had always treated me like an equal and shown interest in my thoughts and activities. My kind, fun, and eccentric sister was gone. There was no way for us to know whether she had made it across, whether she was OK, or even alive.

People communicated from the Austrian refugee camps by coded messages that were transmitted with the help of the Red Cross on the radio. I spent many hours glued to the radio, but never caught anything amid the hundreds of cryptic personal messages that could have been referring to our Márta.

We kept hearing of people in our neighborhood leaving for the border, rumors of thousands leaving the city, trying to escape even though the border was shut down again, the barbed wire in place, guarded by soldiers with machine guns. From my mother's student Alex we found out that her other two engineering students had left. Then we heard that two more of her students, including her beloved Suzie, were gone. But we didn't know for sure whether any of them had made it or perhaps were in jail or even dead. I wanted us to try to escape too. What I would be leaving behind didn't cross my mind, only that if we got to Austria we could go to the United States where my mother's sister Mila and her Aunt Edith lived. Mother was tempted but afraid. Every day we talked it over and weighed the decision as we kept hearing of opportunities in the neighborhood, of a truck that was leaving at 2:00 am, or that so and so had room in another truck the next day. The trains started running again and those heading westward were jam-packed. We were in a constant state of indecision until finally Mother concluded that her face was so transparent, she wouldn't be able to lie if we encountered police or soldiers who asked us where we were headed. If she told them we were going to visit someone in some city close to the border, her face or voice would give her away. As the days passed the opportunities dwindled, until the iron curtain was once again firmly in place.

Although disarmed, Hungarians did not lie down quietly. Somehow the fear that made us docile until 1953 could no longer be invoked. Strikes were called. Demands for the withdrawal of Soviet troops continued. On the afternoon of November 23rd the streets of Budapest became deserted for the first month's anniversary of the revolution. The workers councils that had been established in those few days of freedom continued operating for a while. The new government was hard put to disband them as it was difficult to argue that they were anti-worker, something the whole revolution was being accused of. But finally in December the council heads were arrested, too, and the waves of arrests and reprisals, the rumors of torture and deportation, and the hopelessness of the situation slowly quieted the country. History was rewritten: the uprising had been a counter-revolution of fascist forces, and the heroic people had put it down.

We sank into a bleak normalcy. The tanks remained at the bridge heads and other strategic points until sometime in January, and after that first time, I got used to the tank's gun shaft with its black mouth gaping so near to the bus window, though I tried not to sit on that side. But the stores had food again and school resumed. We were a subdued bunch, shyly exchanging stories of our experiences, again not quite trusting who was who.

The Red Cross was allowed to bring news from the Austrian refugee camps. We learned that Márta had made the crossing and was hoping to go to Paris, having always loved all things French. Peter Halász was okay too, heading to Australia. Suzie, was fine, expecting to eventually go to England. At least 200,000 Hungarian (out of ten million) abandoned their country during that short period. Austria mounted a heroic effort to house and feed the refugees and process them through to the countries that were willing to take them.

In a gesture of good will and practicality, the government decided that old people could apply for exit visas if they had a permit to immigrate from another country. Móri, who was 65 and very frail, applied immediately to go to England to join her son and daughter. In less than two months she received permission to leave, and her children sent a plane ticket. It felt like I was losing my grandmother all over again. By then I knew that she had been a god-send to me, a steady, even-tempered and good-humored presence. We loved each other. When we said our teary goodbye at the airport it was with an understanding that we would never see each other again.

Leaving

Despite the brutal reprisals and the execution of Imre Nagy and other leaders after the revolution failed, Kádár turned out to be a more practical leader rather than an ideological one. Although the dictatorship was restored and terrible reprisals occurred, there was no return to Stalinism, and small enterprises and farms were allowed to continue, creating a more acceptable life for the general population. The government also reevaluated the country's hermetically sealed borders. Why (they may have reasoned) force people to stay in Hungary if they were of no special use? Maybe if some of the folk ready to retire left Budapest, the housing shortage would ease up and the government would save money on their pensions. Whatever the government's reasoning, Móri was allowed to leave, so it was possible to obtain exit visas. Trudi kept pushing my mother to apply. She was fifty years old, close to retirement age (fifty-five for women), and I was still a child to be educated. Maybe the government would be glad to be rid of us. I remember overhearing Trudi and my mother talking; "Do it for her sake," Trudi insisted, meaning me, "Do it for her education." I was in 7th grade and had just one more year of elementary school. High schools were still scarce and priority was still given to children of worker background. "It may take many more years, if ever, for a child of two college graduates to gain a seat," Trudi insisted.

My mother was very apprehensive at the idea of starting a new life in a new place at age fifty. Besides, where could we go? We wanted to go to the United States, where my aunt Mila and great aunt Edith lived with their husbands, and where Mila's son, my only cousin (none of whom I had ever met) lived. The US had taken thousands of refugees who had escaped from Hungary, but going legally was another matter. A quota system determined how many immigrants from each country they would take each year, and in 1957 Hungarians faced a ten-year wait. So where could we go?

It dawned on my mother that Caracas, Venezuela, was an option. That's where, with Father's help, his cousin Ruza and her two daughters had gone in 1948, and now with both daughters married they were doing well. Worn down by Trudi's insistence, Mother wrote to them and much faster than we dreamed Vera, aunt Ruza's older daughter, replied in a telegram asking for the information she needed to arrange for an immigration visa. Practically before we really comprehended what we were doing, a big, official-looking envelope brought us the permits to immigrate to Venezuela.

It was time to apply for an exit visa from Hungary. With reluctance and fear, and with excitement, my mother got the papers together. She never loved Hungary so leaving the country did not concern her. She did, however, love her work and her friends, and she had created a place for herself.

Besides, Budapest was a known evil and who knew what waited for us in South America? Her resolve wavered, but Trudi didn't let her talk herself out of it. The enthusiasm for leaving that I had felt during the days of the revolution, when I was caught up in the excitement of so many people escaping to the West, had waned. I couldn't imagine what it would be like to emigrate. Leaving behind everything I knew, everything I loved, and everything I hated seemed unreal, too big to comprehend. My protests were hushed with recriminations of ingratitude, because after all, I was told, it was for my benefit that my mother was willing to try it. So, with Trudi's determined prodding, we submitted the exit visa application in late February 1957.

After we submitted the papers, life became a limbo. We had no idea whether we would get the visa and didn't want anyone to know that we were even thinking about it until it was a sure thing. I told Eta because I had to discuss it with someone and knew she would not tell anyone if I asked her not to. She thought it was an exciting opportunity for me, but was also stunned and teary. We had become closer than sisters and had planned our whole future life around each other. We clung together at the thought of separation and promised that if I actually did leave, we would write to each other forever. Still, I couldn't actually believe or comprehend the possibility of our leaving, of what it would mean.

I continued attending seventh grade, escaping into math, literature, grammar, and history, but not feeling part of the class. By this our third year together, the class had cohesion and camaraderie. Yet after the incident with

Aunt Maria I ceased to trust in wholehearted friendship with any of them other than Eta, even though I had known some for seven years. None of them was Jewish that I knew of, though some may too have been hiding it. After all, as far as I could tell no one knew about me either, though I couldn't be sure. Anyway, thinking that I might be leaving them soon made me feel even less emotional attachment.

Sometime after Easter a notification came in the mail that our application was rejected. We were dazed, both relieved and disappointed, but before we had a chance to get used to the idea of staying, we got a phone call from a woman asking to come to our apartment to talk about our visa. My mother was mystified but agreed. Next evening a short and stocky, mousy woman arrived and explained that she worked at the passport office and could get us our visa. What she wanted in return was our apartment. She lived in a room in her parents' apartment and needed her own place as she was getting married. Housing in Budapest was still woefully short. She thought our place would be perfect and asked us to think it over and let her know within two days. That was how everything worked in 1950s Hungary, so we shouldn't have been surprised. She probably had investigated our circumstances and purposefully denied our application so she could extort our apartment from us.

The apartment, actually a condominium, was small enough that it hadn't been taken away by the state. Mother owned half and Eva and Márta each owned a quarter. Márta, of course, wasn't there to consult. But in a family council with Trudi and Eva, both supported the idea, saying this was probably the only way we could get an exit visa.

So my mother called the woman back and agreed, and was assured that we would get the visa in two weeks.

A week later the passport woman called again, this time in utter panic. One of the periodic anti-corruption campaigns ("let's have government employees who are 100% above reproach") was starting up. About 90 percent of the population were government employees, virtually every worker other than small artisans and shopkeepers, and those who dared made their lives easier by using the opportunities their jobs afforded. The anti-corruption campaigns were mostly propaganda efforts that nobody believed would be effective or lasting, but some people had to be made an example of. The woman was afraid of getting caught, paraded as an example of corruption, and jailed. She promised us we would get our exit visa, and we could keep our apartment. She begged Mother not to acknowledge her in any way when she picked up the visa and to deny knowing her if she were asked. My mother agreed, of course, as panic stricken as the woman herself. Would we be implicated if this woman were caught? Would we be jailed as part of the corruption? It felt like we were on a roller-coaster that just wouldn't stop.

In a couple of days my mother got a notification in the mail that she was to go to the Interior Ministry office to pick up the "exit passport" five days hence. Instead of rejoicing, she spent five black days imagining all the horrible things that could happen if she were implicated in that woman's scheme. On the appointed day we took the bus to the Oktogon Square. My mother did not want me to come to the building, so we walked slowly to the nearby Jókai

Square and sat on a bench. After a quiet while Mother told me to stay there and that if she didn't return in an hour to go to Trudi's. As she kissed me goodbye, I think we both had visions of prison bars closing and of our never seeing each other again. I know I did. I sat on the sunny bench frozen, suspended, not really daring to think. It seemed an eternity but it was less than half an hour before my mother came back jubilant, with two exit visas in her purse. She was never questioned, and we never saw that woman or heard from her again.

A fairyland-tapestry of freedom and luxury, braided tightly with heartbreak, covered the next five months. The document my mother signed in order to get the exit visa was a renunciation of our Hungarian citizenship. She gladly did so. But I loved my country helplessly, even as I understood that it didn't consider me a real Hungarian. I was fed by its air, by its earth and what grew there and by the stories of its heroes. In my yearning to belong I had no other place that I could imagine belonging to but this country, this city that I was about to leave probably for ever and that contained all the people I loved.

We sold the apartment for one million forints to a fiftyish, stooped, bespectacled stranger. So there was money in Hungary, just not in our circle. We were lucky and found Dr. Tamasko, a wonderful attorney, whom my mother promptly rechristened "Angel." He did all the arrangements. Márta's share went to Eva, and we ended up with 500,000 forints. That represented the equivalent of what my mother would earn in eight years—unimaginable riches. Ironically, we couldn't take any of it with us. It was play money anywhere but in Hungary and the Eastern Bloc, because Hungary's currency was not tradable in the West. Trudi and Miklós would have an easier life with most of our share and I was very glad of that. But for five months we lived well.

Small businesses and shops thrived, and we were able to have the clothes that we would take with us custom made. Good food, though expensive, was more and more available. Now we could afford it and took advantage of it, going to my favorite Honey Bear for little sandwiches and other goodies and to the Gerbaud, the marvelous and before the war famous pastry shop in Vörösmarty Square, right where Eva lived, where I tasted the pastries I could only look at longingly the last couple of years. Trudi took me to the Ruszwurm, Budapest's oldest pastry shop in the old Castle district, once the most beautiful district but then not yet repaired from the ravages of the war, its buildings sporting bullet holes instead of heralds. But that didn't prevent me from savoring their magnificent poppy seed strudel and chocolate balls, and my time with Trudi.

And so I experienced the luxuries, the salami, the biscuits with cracklings, sweets, and the new shoes, and the not having to worry about money. Yet often I filled my stomach to squeeze out of it the anxiety, and the treats left a bitter aftertaste. What I was leaving behind slowly sank in, and every person, every place became more luminous, more precious.

My adored Aunt Trudi. My lovely, exotic, temperamental sister. Her son, Gábor, the sweet, though often intimidating large teddy bear. My friend Eta. The inhabitants of

Csévi Street 3, who were my extended family. Our quiet third-floor neighbors, Mr. and Mrs. Füredi and all their wonderful books. Kind Mr. Gerlei and beautiful Mrs. Gerlei with her upswept hair and serene smile, and Ferkó, their tall 18-year-old son with beautiful black eyes, with whom I was totally infatuated. Anti, who had been my pal since we were toddlers and his parents, Uncle Réfi, gruff and kind, and Aunt Réfi, always there, always good-naturedly tolerating my hanging about. I stared lovingly at them all. It was incomprehensible that I would have to leave them forever. Returning for visits never entered my mind, aware of the cost and distance and above all of those impenetrable borders.

Hearing the strains of haunting folk music played in the ramshackle house next to us, my soul rode on the notes back to a past where, I fervently believed, Hungary was noble and I belonged to it and in it. My head knew this place had never existed, but my heart knew that it did. Smelling the lilac blooms on the hedge that separated our building from the next one, I tried to infuse my lungs with its fragrance, convinced that I'd never breathe that smell again.

Classes ended, and I knew I wasn't going to eighth grade with the group. As soon as my classmates knew I wasn't returning, what little remained of the closeness I felt with a few of the girls vanished. I sensed their envy and a closing of ranks. The little interlude of feeling like I actually might belong was long over, but this new level of isolation made my heart ache anew. Only with Eta did I spend time that last summer. We walked around arm in arm, talking about our dreams of becoming teachers, wondering whom we would marry, what life in unimaginable South America would be like, promising eternal friendship.

Wandering around the neighborhood, I tried to memorize my favorite buildings, trees, streets. Riding the number 5 bus I tried to fix in my memory as much as I could. Taking the tram to Széna Square, I found the chestnut trees more lovely than ever, and even the dirty, bullet-hole-ridden buildings seemed beautiful. Walking along to Trudi's, I caressed the remnants of the old city wall. I was in love with all of my city.

I went to Trudi's often and sat for her as she sculpted a bust of me from clay. Though I had to keep my head still, I looked at her, and drank in her features, wondering whether I would forget them. The tips of her long fingers all were cracked from working in clay and plaster and washing them so often. I tried to rub lotion into them, but it didn't seem to make any difference. After sitting we would have lunch and she and Miklós would tease me, trying to make me see that I was embarking on a very exciting adventure. I just couldn't imagine life without them.

I didn't want to leave without seeing Lake Balaton again, so my mother agreed for us to go to Balatonszemes for four days. It wasn't the same without staying in the villa with Aunt Klári and the other kids as I had a couple of years before, but at least I was there, walked my favorite paths, waded in a bit, and sat on the pier watching the beautiful sunset. I knew that no matter how many beautiful and interesting places I would see in my new life, none could be as lovely as the sunset on the Balaton was that day.

We had to decide what to take with us, realizing that

we were starting a new life and would not be able to afford to buy things for a while. Partly our choices were made for us because the government prescribed what was allowed: one coat and one raincoat each, four dresses, two skirts, three blouses, one swim suit, and so on. The good thing was that we could afford to have good quality dresses, coats, and shoes made. We were allowed to take exactly eight sheets, two pillows, and so forth. Although good quality new things were important, our first criterion was sentimental value, so we took a tablecloth embroidered by my grandmother, sheets my father used, and handkerchiefs with Grandmami's monograms.

The paintings by Miklós that we wanted to take with us had to be approved. Although he hardly could sell any of his wonderful artwork, the government declared the paintings a "national treasure" and granted permission for only six of the paintings we owned. Among the 45 books we could take, my mother allowed me to choose two of my father's favorites, especially precious to me and two books he sometimes read to me, so long ago. I also took my Hungarian missal. Along with two photo albums, we were allowed twelve small items of "family memorabilia." I chose the almost disintegrated teddy bear my father gave me on my second birthday and one of his tennis balls, which I treasured. My heart grew more and more numb as we kept paring down. Looking at every single object we owned, we had to decide whom to give it to, or whether to leave it with Trudi for some unfathomable future time.

My mother couldn't bring herself to part with one special piece of jewelry, a beautiful platinum pendant with a pearl in the middle and a cluster of small diamonds. My grandmother and she both wore it on their wedding day and she was determined that I should too. Smuggling it out was too risky; we had heard frightful stories about people getting caught. Mother also had several items of costume jewelry that she wanted to take, all of which needed to be approved and sealed in a bag by some petit bureaucrat, so our lawyer came up with a suggestion. He threaded the beautiful pendant onto a gaudy beady necklace and include it in the bag, which he would take in for approval. As luck would have it, when he presented the contents of the bag the pendant landed upside down, with only its plain tarnished back showing. The bored and tired bureaucrat, looked over the handful of bijou without careful examination and told the lawyer to put it all back, closing the bag with a permit seal. We purchased two trunks and packed them in front of an official holding a clip-board checking off the allowed items. Then they were sealed by a government seal to be put on the train.

Hungary was a closed world and nothing of what was going to happen once we crossed the border could be arranged from within. Even as we were completing all these preparations, we had no idea how we were going to get to Caracas. Then about three weeks before we were due to leave, a charming letter arrived from a travel agent in Italy complete with train tickets from the border to Genoa, reservations at a pension there, boat tickets from Genoa to Caracas, arrangement for our trunks, and careful instructions for accomplishing all.

Mother gave me a pretty little keepsake album, and I

passed it around to my special people to write remembrances for me. There wasn't sufficient time so I collected many fewer than I had hoped, but I still treasure the ones I have.

The goodbyes strung out over weeks with the hardest ones left until the end. We visited my father's cousin uncle Andrew, and Aunt Böske, who was Karola's sweet sister and at whose home we had always celebrated Eva's birthday. We went to the cemetery and sat by Grandmami's grave, covered with the white and purple flowers that she loved. Then we went to Father's grave. Its rough white surface, with only his name and small interlocking white marble squares across the middle, always made me think of a knight's tomb. Saying goodbye to him there unloosened another bit of tie to him. I felt cold and empty even though it was a bright fall day. A last dinner at Eva's and goodbye to Gábor. A last walk with Eta, both of us crying and making promises.

The evening of our departure finally arrived. A last look around the apartment, the room we had lived in through all those years, the bed and armoires that I thought so beautiful, Father's desk. It was all going to strangers. Carrying just our purses and an overnight bag, accompanied by Mr. and Mrs. Gerlei, the entire Réfi family, and my beloved friend Eta, we walked the two minutes to the terminal of the number 5 bus in Pasaréti Square. One more hug, one more kiss, one more promise to keep in touch, and we climbed on to the waiting bus, driven by one of my friends.

The bus started round the circle, everyone waving. As I leaned slightly to offset the bus's momentum, I felt my heart tear and saw a piece of it severed and floating backwards, not leaving with me. It stayed with my beloved people, my beloved house, my beloved square that I knew I would never see again. I was leaving everything I knew and that was dear to me, and it no longer felt like an adventure. It was a tearing so painful it felt like death.

We weren't going to the train station just yet, but to Trudi's for a last dinner before our very late train. I sobbed all the way as we rode on the bus and then walked the few blocks on Martyrs Avenue to number 58. Trudi made my favorite meal, creamed spinach with a fried egg on top and boiled potatoes, then cottage cheese filled crepes. But I was too overwrought to eat. Finally the time came to say goodbye to Uncle Miklós and get a taxi to the train station. Miklós, wearing his eternal white doctor's coat to protect his clothes from paint, was joking, trying to make me smile, but I could see through it to his heart. Trudi came to the train station with us, embracing me in the taxi and murmuring encouragements, reminding me that I had to be very good.

At the train station Aunt Nusi (Mrs. Halász) and my sister Eva were waiting to say goodbye. I shivered uncontrollably from the cold and emotional exhaustion. Words of encouragement all around, perhaps even of envy, were spoken—after all we were leaving for the land of possibilities. But that is not how it felt to me. A last hug, Trudi pinching my bottom, her unemotional teasing love always bracing. Climbing onto the train, and peering out the window, my last picture was Trudi with her batik scarf tied back on her head, her long brown coat, and the eternal silver rope strand around her neck, waving and sending kisses as the train pulled out.

I cried myself to sleep as we rolled through the night. At Hegyeshalom, the border town, soldiers with machine guns boarded the train, forcing us all out with our luggage while they searched the train. It was a cold, damp, windy October night, with only the couple of dozen emigrants left on the platform waiting to reboard the train. Our luggage was sealed in Budapest, so the soldiers checked only that the seals were unbroken and searched our purses and overnight bag.

Then while the rest waited shivering on the cold platform, we each had to go in, one by one. I heard the others muttering that everyone was going to be searched. My turn came and I was waved into a small room where a heavy-set uniformed woman told me to take all my clothes off. After carefully examining every piece of clothing, I was horrified to have her slide her hands over me and inside me, making

My photograph in the exit visa from Hungary.

sure no jewels were hidden for us to take out illegally. I remember nothing more until we got to Vienna the next morning.

My country's goodbye was not sweet, but then my country was never sweet to me. Yet it was my country. Even as it disowned me, it formed me and put its indelible stamp on me: Made in Hungary.

Epilogue

We spent seven difficult years in Venezuela, including my high school years. It was a closed society, and in the seven years I was never invited to a native Venezuelan's home. There was a large Hungarian community, a microcosm of Hungary with all the social patterns transferred plus some unique divisions added between those who came before the war, after the war, and in 1956. The major division was that of Jews and Christians, roughly equally represented. The Jewish community wouldn't welcome us because we were not practicing Jews, and therefore somewhat viewed as traitors. Besides, my mother looked upon our landing in a strange country as one more firewall between us and the danger of being known as Jews. So we tried the Christian Hungarians, many of whom had left between 1945 and 1948, and fled fearing reprisals because of their Nazi activities or because they foresaw the tightening control by the communists. This group proved impossible for us, as they devotedly went to Mass and spewed anti-Semitic remarks even while in church. One try was enough.

So we went to church with other Venezuelans and slowly found some friends both among European Jews and

Christians. They all lived as expatriates and it was clear that was all we would ever be. Even after we became citizens (for five years we were stateless), we were always referred to as "the *naturalized* citizen so and so..." While we were there the country suffered a coup d'etat, followed by unchecked violence and continuous crime sprees. I could never warm to the country or feel at home there.

In 1963, we finally were able to save sufficient money to come to the United States to visit Mother's sister and aunt. I started to work in 1960, at age 16, and also competed at a TV tic-tac-dough quiz show and won a sum of money that covered our airfare. My mother's sister Mila had visited us in Caracas, but it would be my first time to meet my only cousin and great aunt. It was a beautiful day in early May when we landed at Idlewild Airport in New York (today JFK) and there was fragrance wafting from nearby flowering trees. It smelled like home. By the time we got into Manhattan I had told my mother "I am moving here and I don't care what it takes!" That my greataunt looked and acted like Trudi was an important added draw.

Providence was with us. The immigration quota system had been recently changed, and Mother having a sister here put us on a faster track. My cousin John found a friend willing to guarantee that we would never be a financial burden on the state, and so it was possible for us to receive our green cards and arrive as immigrants in June of 1964. When we saw the banner reading "Welcome to America!" as we walked toward customs, we both burst out crying and I held Mother back from kneeling down and kissing the ground.

This book is not the story of my forty-some years in the United States, but some things about my life here bear saying. The "Welcome to America" sign at the airport did not lie. I know that not everyone is or has been welcome here, but personally I never felt anything but. People still ask me "Where are you from?" But they are only curious about my accent, which I could never lose, and the response has always been one of interest without a shadow of the reserve that I had gotten so good at detecting. After a few years I threw off my mother's fears and openly acknowledged my Jewish heritage. I continued to be a Catholic and later became a Quaker, but I learned to publicly own, to understand, to love, and to be proud of my heritage. Yet my pride is often still mingled with gut-wrenching grief remembering the past and seeing what is happening in the Middle East—how Jews continue to suffer but have also become perpetrators of suffering. After six years in the States, I became a US citizen and have not once felt that I was a second-class citizen. I know with certainty that as an American I am free to participate in all aspects of life and to contribute to make the US an ever better, more just society.

I feel at home here. I am grateful for and love the United States, and the principles upon which it was founded. I have wonderful friends and an American-born, all-American son. I learned civics and American history, and read American literature. So why don't I still feel like I unequivocally belong? Sometimes I almost do, and then someone will mention a children's story, or talk about their school experiences and the illusion vanishes. I love Thanksgiving and the Fourth of July, but when I sit around the table or the barbecue and sense what these holidays mean to those around me, I know they are not truly mine.

In 1971, fourteen years after I left Hungary, I returned to Budapest for the first time. I hugged my US passport like a security blanket, especially when faced again with uniformed soldiers toting machine guns at the border. This was still communist Hungary, though I found it incredibly freer and better off than I had left it. Seeing Trudi and Eva again was pure joy, as was eating some of my favorite foods. The places I had enshrined in memory seemed so much smaller but still held their charm for me. I eagerly went to all my special spots, finding that much had changed and much remained the same. Family and friends laughingly accused me of speaking Hungarian with a foreign accent. On the same visit I went to England and saw Móri once more.

I have gone back to visit a few more times, once taking my American son with me. Witnessing continued changes for both the better and the worse, I have felt more and more removed and yet not. Hungary is the land and the people who didn't want me, wanted to kill me, yet even in their rejection they did form me. It is the land that fed me, whose fruits and flowers enchanted me. These are the people whose lullabies and children's ditties spoke to me, whose heroes fueled my imagination.

I am not "cured" of Hungary, no matter how much I'd like to be. My unrequited love affair still continues, mostly quiescent, but it can be awakened unexpectedly by the smell of lilacs or jasmine, a flowering chestnut tree, a conversation about salami. Then I close my eyes and I am in Csévi

Street or Pasaréti Square, at the Chain Bridge, or some other forever magical place. And I let the longing wash over me, the longing to be all of one piece, to know that I unquestionably, totally belong. But then I smile and know that although I was made in Hungary, I am an American woman who speaks four languages, but none without an accent.

The Author's Family

Alexander Fleischl
(later Felhös) father

Andy Falusi
Eva's second husband

Bertha Schulz
maternal grandmother
(Grandmami)

Endre Kálmán
Eva's third husband

Eva Kálmán
half-sister

Gábor Holzmann
Eva and Willie's son, my
nephew

Gene (Jenö) Kovács
Trudi's first husband

Julius Donner
maternal grandfather

Izso Fleischl
paternal grandfather

Karl Feldmann
(later Bodo) Mila's
husband

Karola Gyenes
father's first wife, Eva &
Márta's mother

Laura Stux
paternal grandmother

Marianne Donner
mother

Márta Gerber
half-sister

Miklós Farkasházy
Trudi's second husband,
well-known painter

Mila Bodo
mother's eldest sister

Móri (Mária Bérczi)
adopted grandmother

Trudi (Gertrude)
Farkasházy
mother's middle sister

Willie Holzmann
Eva's first husband

LaVergne, TN USA
03 October 2010
199406LV00001B/1/P